St. Gemma Galgani

St. Gemma Galgani

St. Gemma Galgani

THE RT. REV. DR. LEO PROSERPIO, S.J.

BISHOP OF CALICUT

WITH A FOREWORD BY

HIS EXCELLENCY THE MOST REV.
DR. LEO PETER KIERKELS, C.P.

APOSTOLIC DELEGATE TO THE EAST INDIES

Revenir Books

Tucson, Arizona

2022

Nihil Obstat:
H.B. Ries
Censor librorum

Imprimatur:
Samuel A. Stritch
Archiepiscopus Milwaukiensis
February 27, 1940

Originally Published by
Bruce Publishing Company, Milwaukee
1940

Republished in paperback
Revenir Books
Tucson, Arizona
January, 2022

Cover Art:
Beautiful photomechanical prints of Lotus Flowers
Ogawa Kazumasa
1887–1897

Cover Design:
Revenir Books

ISBN: 9798402543317

Contents

Preface by the General Editor

The life of Gemma Galgani, the Maid of Lucca, is God's own reply to the materialism of her day and ours. Her few years on earth, for she died in the early flowering of her youth, were cast in an age of unbelief. It was the last quarter of the nineteenth century and the opening of the twentieth. The seeds then sown are now being harvested.

To realize properly the condition of those days we need but turn to the Encyclicals of Pope Leo XIII, all of which were written during precisely that entire period.

Slight note, we can well understand, was there given to the presence among men of a rare and wonderful soul, of one around whom Divine Providence was weaving even then the marvels of another world. Gemma Galgani. Her name is the laughter of God in His heavens at the folly of men who deny Him on earth:

> He that is throned in the Heavens mocks them,
> The Lord laughs them to scorn.

Here, indeed, was a being whose whole life brings us into intimate and realistic touch with the supernatural. The world of spirit lay close to her, was made visible and tangible to her. Here was one in whose daily life transpired things mystic and mysterious, things inexplicable alike to mere human learnings and experimental science. Yet of the facts there is no doubt. Reason must acknowledge them. Science accept them, but Faith alone can attempt to explain them.

So now, to the marvels of Lourdes, attested by strictest medical research, to the symbolic shower of roses, confidently predicted by St. Thérèse and continuing steadily to fall throughout all the years since her death; to the innumerable other transcendent events, must be added the mystic experiences of Gemma Galgani, interestingly and convincingly narrated in this book, with due regard to all scientific aspects.

Appearing simultaneously with the performance of the brilliant rites in Vatican City, whereby the glory of canonized sainthood encircles the brows of the lowly Maid of Lucca, this volume comes to us from the hand of a Jesuit Bishop in distant India, an ardent client himself of the humble Saint, and worthily prefaced by the stately words dedicated to her honor by His Excellency, the Apostolic Delegate of the East Indies.

So the ends of the earth have arisen to do her homage and the anointed of the Lord have proclaimed her praises who on earth was a penniless waif, dependent on Christian charity, and dying in the home of a stranger. A pauper child, but oh, how tenderly, visibly, familiarly, loved by Christ and her Guardian Angel and the Holy Mother of God!

In the midst of a materialistic civilization, whose vaunted progress has failed, her life stands out for all the world to see, as the triumph of the supernatural.

Joseph Husslein, S.J., Ph.D.
General Editor, Science and Culture Series
St. Louis University,
February 27, 1940

Foreword

Among God's saints there are some who more than others remind us that not only is mankind "little less than the angels," but that the children of men may be on earth "like God's angels in heaven," nay almost superior to the celestial spirits, since they are by virtue and choice what the angels are by nature and necessity. Such a saint is Gemma Galgani of whom it has been said as of St. Agnes that "even her name constitutes a praise." She is indeed a *gem* of Christian virtue and purity, who like St. Aloysius "united a wonderful innocence with equal penance" and mortification, to which Divine Providence added so many sufferings and trials that she has fittingly been called *lilium inter spinas* — a lily among thorns. Her humbly heroic life and virtues are indeed worthy of the episcopal pen which enhances a subject so edifying and inspiring in itself.

Monsignor Proserpio's work constitutes a most interesting addition to the literature on the subject. We have Gemma's autobiography, written under obedience, and her Letters, the informative Proceedings of the several ecclesiastical and Roman courts, the Lives written by Father Williamson, Sister Gesualda, Father Amedeo, and above all the Life written by Father Germano. This latter's work, translated into many languages, is especially valuable, not only because, as Gemma's spiritual director, he had such an intimate knowledge of her soul, but also because his books on scientific subjects and his high standing in Roman Academies and learned circles are a guarantee of his critical exactness. In fact, in the informative Proceedings he deposed his entire biography of Gemma under oath. But Bishop Proserpio has successfully aimed at giving a novel interest to the edifying life of our heroine and I trust that it will reach an ever wider sphere of readers.

Indeed the life of St. Gemma Galgani is not meant only for the edification, and incitement to pious emulation, of a limited number of devotees and admirers. In the Decree proclaiming her heroic virtues, the Holy See indicated a wider viewpoint in considering her historic role and significance. She is proposed as an object lesson against secularism and irreligion, as an affirmation before the world of the Christian outlook on life and eternity. That role she only virtually fulfilled during her earthly life, since but a small group of privileged persons were aware of her inner greatness. Humble and unnoticed by the world at large, she passed through a remarkable period of history, in which the Catholic attention was held by the great Pope Leo XIII, with whose pontificate the mortal career of the humble Maid of Lucca practically coincides. But today the parts are, so to say, reversed and it is St. Gemma Galgani who, from the glory of our altars, proclaims the Catholic viewpoint and spirit which inspired the Pontiff in whose reign she lived her hidden life. Of course, she had only a limited field for the practical application of the principles which the great Pope endeavored to render paramount in every sphere of human activity. But the Catholic faith and attitude permeated her whole life, and that is just what Leo XIII aimed at obtaining: the permeation of the world by the Catholic faith and mind.

However, as in the case of most saints, Gemma's life emphasizes a particular aspect of our faith and religion. The Holy See's pronouncements stress that she is to be considered as a spiritual daughter of St. Paul of the Cross, that she assimilated his spirit, and that his example and teachings were the norm of her spiritual life: *quem veluti ejus sanctitatis ducem ac magistrum merito dixeris* — who rightly may be regarded as her guide and teacher. In fact one of the outstanding characteristics of Gemma's sanctity is her devotion to Jesus Crucified, which from a particular angle embraces our entire Holy Religion, since, in the words of a pious writer "Our whole Religion is comprised in Christ Crucified." Thus Gemma proclaims "by example rather than by words," the message of the Cross, and with the great Apostle she may profess not to have known anything but Jesus Christ and Him Crucified, or as another Roman document expresses it: "There stands forth, delightful to the eyes of all, that fair example of life, whereby this lowly maid taught Christ and Him Crucified to a world that is declining into vanity."[1]

May the readers of this holy Life fully realize St. Gemma's testimonium Christi — her witnessing to Christ, and may her spiritual and mystic greatness fire many souls with zeal and fervor for the fulfillment of that message in themselves and in our harassed world! May St. Gemma's prayers obtain for individuals and nations "the peace of Christ in the reign of Christ."

Leo P. Kierkels, C.P.
Apostolic Delegate
Bangalore, India

Introduction

O n Holy Saturday, April 11, 1903, whilst the bells of many churches were pealing forth the last joyous notes of the resurrection, a young maiden passed peacefully away in one of the provincial towns of Italy. To the few friends, kneeling around her deathbed, she was an "angel" in human form, whom a benevolent Providence had sent down from the heavenly mansions to sanctify their homes. To the people at large, in the neighborhood, she was but a servant maid of whom very strange things were told. For years they had looked upon her suspiciously; they had alternately honored her as a saint and reviled her as a witch and a deceiver. Did any of them foresee that the girl, who lay a-dying, would soon be revered on the altars of the Church because her life, totally hidden with Christ in God, had reflected in a most marvelous manner some ray of the Eternal Beauty?

Looking back thirty years into the past, Pius XI, after reading the decree that proclaimed heroic the virtue of the holy Maid of Lucca, said in an allocution to the Cardinals: "What has happened today is something greater and more remarkable than what ordinarily happens. It has come about in God's own way. He exalts the humble and makes them first in His Kingdom." Then, though he had known her only by sight, the Holy Father added:

"I can see her once more before me, dressed in black, wearing her *mantellette*, not very tall, light of step, almost silent, with a transfigured face, with sweet and soft large eyes made to see immortal things.

"Comparing her figure, which I keep alive and present in my mind, with her portrait, I find my recollection to be true. That face, luminous and peaceful, remains and will remain in my mind and heart as the face of a saint. Who would have thought at the time, when a heated controversy was waging around this girl, and people alternately sided for and against her — even though her virtue was ever held in high esteem — who would have thought of today's triumph and of the great things Divine Providence reserves for the morrow?"

These words of Pius XI, with that prophetic ring in their concluding sentence, made the clients of Gemma Galgani hope that soon they would see the day of her complete triumph in canonization. That triumphant day has come, but the great Pontiff, who foresaw and looked forward to its realization, is no more.

Gemma's canonization has aroused an intense wave of enthusiasm throughout the length and breadth of Italy, her native land. She is the first tribute of the twentieth century to the God of sanctity — a maid of childlike simplicity, of passionate love for Jesus Crucified, of angelic purity, and of sublime prayer, though hidden away in obscurity. These seem to be characteristic features in the lives of modern saints. Defense of the Faith unto blood, it is true, has been witnessed anew in many countries where men and women have given up their lives with the cry upon their lips, "Long live Christ the King!" But so, too, there is still that living martyrdom of holy souls who, like Thérèse of Lisieux, Gemma Galgani, and a host of others, gain by hidden suffering, by continuous prayer and mortification, a crown of glory not less resplendent than that of the martyrs.

As His Excellency, the Delegate Apostolic to the East Indies, has here pointed out in his Preface, the life of St. Gemma coincides with the pontificate of Leo XIII. She was born in 1878, shortly after his election, and died in April, 1903, a few months before the Pope's death. It was an age of comparative peace in Church and State during which, however, the progress of science, the forward movement of industrial capitalism, as well as secular education, were paving the way for the universal unrest of modern days.

The present writer has deliberately excluded from his narrative all references to the historical background of our Saint's life. Gemma was not a Catherine of Siena nor a Vincent de Paul. From the point of view of external influence few lives of saints have reacted so little on contemporary events as that of Gemma Galgani. Hers was a hidden life. It has often been compared with that of St. Thérèse of Lisieux, whose rainfall of mystical roses gladdens the world. The two Saints are indeed twin sisters in more ways than one. They were contemporaries; they both lived the same number of years, and both died young. They were raised to the altars soon after death, although the Little Flower, born five years earlier, had a more speedy and greater glorification. Indeed, up to the age of fifteen the two Saints are extraordinarily similar in charm and innocence of life. At that age Marie Francoise Thérèse Martin became Soeur Thérèse de l'Enfant Jesus in the Carmel of Lisieux where, with ineffable grace, she continued to teach simple souls the simple way of love. At nearly the same age Gemma, too, knocks at the gate of the convent, but knocks in vain, though her efforts to obtain admission are continued to the end of her days. Instead, she was to spend her last years in the home of strangers, an orphan maid, and fastened, like St. Paul, to the cross of Christ.

The story of Gemma Galgani's life was first published by the Rev. Father Germano of St. Stanislaus, C.P., her spiritual director during the three years she lived in the Giannini household. He did not venture to print more than seven hundred copies of his book. But at the time of Gemma's beatification its diffusion had exceeded one hundred thousand copies, and it had been translated into all the principal languages of Europe. Though perhaps wanting in some historical details, which can be found in more recent biographies, the Life by Father Germano still remains the standard work on our Saint. It is brimful of that unction and deep insight into spiritual things from which is derived the beauty of ancient hagiography. Writers of the psychological school of lives of the saints, with which we nowadays are so familiar, have lost the art of moving the soul. They seem as unable to win it back as the painters of today are incapable of recapturing the rich and soft tints we admire so much in the stained-glass windows of medieval cathedrals.

We wish to take this opportunity to express publicly our admiration and love for this great son of St. Paul of the Cross. In the midst of much uncertainty and opposition he alone was able to judge aright the spirit of the lowly maid of Lucca. He it was who, though hundreds of miles away, undertook to guide her soul at a time when she stood sorely in need of a spiritual director and consoler. But the Saint he guided was not to be lacking in gratitude to him. In his work, *Letters and Ecstasies of Gemma Galgani*, Father Germano published a letter written him by Gemma in which the following words occur: "You will see what I shall do when I go to heaven; I will drag you with me at any cost." The good Father appends a footnote stating simply: "I live on this hope. Amidst the labors of my exile here below these words of Gemma shall always be my comfort."

Although such consoling words were never addressed to the writer of the present Life, he confidently hopes that his own volume, undertaken in token of gratitude for many spiritual graces received through her intercession, will prevail on the dear Saint and prompt her to shower new favors upon him, and upon all those who derive from his work love and devotion toward her.

Leo Proserpio, S.J.
Bishop of Calicut

Part One

THE MAID OF LUCCA

1878-1900

Chapter I

LET HER NAME BE GEMMA

G emma Galgani was born on March 12, 1878, in Camigliano, a quiet village, nestling amidst the vineyards at the foot of the pre-Appenine hills, not far from the Tuscan town of Lucca. Her father, Signor Enrico Galgani, was a prosperous pharmacist,[2] and a descendant of Blessed Giovanni Leonardi. Her mother, too, came of a good lineage, being related to the noble house of the Florentine Landi. They were twin souls, conspicuous for their piety and for the noble ideals and aspirations of their life. Both belonged to the class of stanch Catholic families, happily still very numerous in the rural districts and provincial towns of Italy. Gemma was the first of the girls born to the Galganis, whose union was ultimately blessed by God with eight children. One of these, of whom there is no record, died in infancy.[3]

The happy parents welcomed their fourth newborn as a precious gift from the hands of the Lord. They had long prayed for a little girl, and it is no wonder that her coming filled their hearts with unspeakable joy. Like the parents of another great Saint they had married with the avowed purpose of rearing children who would serve God here on earth and enjoy Him forever in life everlasting. Things have greatly changed since that day.

On the day following her birth, the child was brought to the parish church of St. Michael for holy baptism. Here a little incident occurred not dissimilar to that which St. Luke narrates in speaking of the miraculous naming of the Precursor. The brother-in-law of the mother, a medical Officer in the Italian army, wished that the newly born baby should be called Gemma which in English means "gem."

"But why?" exclaimed the pious mother. "There is none of our kindred, and no blessed in heaven, that is called by this name. If we call her Gemma, she will have no patron Saint to take care of her, and we shall never be able to celebrate her day."

The dispute lasted a little while and might have ended in unpleasantness when the parish priest of Gragnano, who was present at the baptism and was a relative of the family, said: "Not so, but let her name be Gemma. Heaven is the place of jewels and precious stones, and who knows but that this little girl may not become a gem of Paradise?" So she was called Gemma and, indeed, if ever in any case a child's name was prophetic, it undoubtedly was in this.

About a month after Gemma's birth, Signor Enrico, in order to provide better for the education of his children, left Camigliano and settled in the town of Lucca, with which town the name of Gemma Galgani is indissolubly associated.

Lucca, the capital of the like-named province in Tuscany, is an ancient city mentioned by Livy as the place to which, in 218 B.C., Sempronius retired before the invading forces of Hannibal. It is situated in the valley of the Serchio and from its fertile, cultivated plain, looks for the most part on a horizon of hills and mountains. Its fortifications ranked of old among the most remarkable in the Italian peninsula. They were built when the town, like most of the industrial cities of medieval Italy, had to be constantly on the watch against the foreign invader for the defense of its civic liberties and the glory of being master of its own commune. They still encircle it within a massive wall, and are well preserved and picturesque, their projecting bastions being planted with big and shady trees. The city, which has an artistic and substantial appearance, is known to tourists for its celebrated

baths, about fifteen miles from the town, and for its oil of world-wide
fame.

But Lucca's chief attraction[4] lies in its numerous churches, all of which
possess valuable works of art. Noteworthy among them is the Cathedral,
dedicated to St. Martin, and dating back to the sixth century. It is built
in the basilican style. Its apse, the arched or domed recess at the altar
end of the church, has three large windows painted by Ugolino da Pisa,
and there are pictures inside by Tintoretto, and a Madonna by Fra Bar-
tolomeo. In the nave there is a little octagonal chapel, which serves as a
shrine for the most precious among the relics of Lucca.

This is an ancient crucifix, carved in cedarwood, with Christ clothed in
a sleeveless royal garment, the *colobium*. His hands and feet are pierced
with nails but there is no title above the head and no crown of thorns.
Tradition ascribes it to Nicodemus. It is evidently a work of the first
centuries of Christianity: those centuries when Christian art, for fear of
shocking and alienating the pagans, refused to show them the Man-God
in an attitude of utter humiliation and chose to add the triumph of Divine majesty to the agonized face of the Crucified. An old legend relates
how it came from Palestine across the sea in a closed boat, steered by
the hands of invisible angels. Preceded on its route by a long series of
miracles, this precious relic finally entered Lucca on Good Friday of
the year 782. It was received at the gate of St. Frediano by the people.
They went forth to meet the coming Christ, as the Jews had met Him
on the slopes of Mount Olivet when they cried: "Hosanna! Blessed is
he that cometh in the name of the Lord, the king of Israel." From this
majestic figure of the Crucified Lucca derives the proud title of *Città del
Volto Santo*, the city of the Holy Face. The *Volto*, or face, is considered
a true likeness of the Savior. From it, too, began that undying devotion
to Jesus Crucified which forms, even now, a strong characteristic of the
citizens of Lucca.

No wonder that Gemma, who grew up in the shadow of that Tree
of the Cross, manifested early, and retained throughout life, an ardent

love for the Passion of Christ. Often, even as a little child, she was seen kneeling before the altar of the precious relic, which centuries of historical associations had made the palladium of her city. In this she was greatly helped by her mother. Aurelia Galgani was not only a devout Catholic but a real saint, and a perfect model of a Christian mother. She was one of those, too few in our days, for whom religion is never a mere external experience, but an influence which molds every thought, feeling, and action from within. Like Catherine, the mother of Don Bosco; like many a holy woman in Christian hagiology, Aurelia Galgani soon became aware that a rare soul had been entrusted to her keeping by the *Volto Santo.*

Chapter II

TELL ME MORE ABOUT JESUS

Before we go forward in the narrative of Gemma Galgani's wonderful life we think it worthwhile to forestall some objections which may perhaps arise in the mind of the reader. The heroine, he might conclude, appears so utterly faultless from the start, so saintly and supernatural, as to leave the impression of being deficient in the best qualities of human nature. Indeed, she has been represented as timid and soulless — a fitting subject for just one more life written with an eye to edification. This objection carries greater weight in view of our present-day tendency to lay stress on the purely natural characteristics of the saints. Recent biographical studies remind us that the saints were high spirited, bright, and cheery; that some of them had even a pronounced liking for sport, and they are inclined more readily to make mention of St. John Bosco, St. Vincent de Paul, and St. Francis Xavier, than an Aloysius or a Berchmans.

No doubt allowance must be made for the change which modern conditions have brought about in our outlook on life and consequently in our psychology of spiritual phenomena. Yet let us never forget that not only does star differ from star, but their infinite variety of form, shape, and beauty far exceeds the narrow calculations of our mind. Each individual saint is ultimately a masterpiece of God's grace. It is this supernatural gift which fulfills in the varied human beings some likeness to the boundless infinitude of traits and virtues which adorn the inexhaustible personality of Christ. In the language of St. Paul, good Christians, and saints in particular, are "an epistle of Christ."[5] These heavenly letters must be thankfully received and read as Christ Himself inspired them, even though their style should, at times, seem to modern taste antiquated and out of fashion, and their life purposeless in our eyes.

The parents of Gemma loved all their children exceedingly and spared no pains in bringing them up according to the old traditions of Catholic Italy. Yet the newly born child held a special place in their hearts. Signor Enrico, in particular, seems to have been a little too partial to his girl. Like the father of St. Thérèse of Lisieux he used to take her out with him in his walks and, whenever this was not possible, his first care on returning home was to inquire after her. Gemma, indeed, felt that this affection of her father was excessive and would at times tell him so, adding with great simplicity she was unworthy of so much love. When, moved by irresistible impulse, he attempted to kiss her, the little one invariably resisted, saying she did not like to be kissed.

"But surely," he would plead, "I am your father."

"Yes, I know, papa, but Jesus tells me I must not be touched and kissed by anyone."

In order not to grieve her, Signor Enrico would let her have her way.

When three years old, Gemma was sent with the other children to a select private school, conducted by the two ladies Vallini. They have given combined testimony to her rare virtue:

"Our dear Gemma was only two years old when she first came to our school. (Contrary to this statement, an aunt of Gemma, Elisa Galgani, who was a second mother to the child, gives her age as three at the time she went to the Vallini.) Her father entrusted her to us for her education. From the first she gave such signs of intelligence as might make one believe that she had already attained the use of reason. She was serious and thoughtful, far beyond her companions of more advanced years. She was never seen to cry or quarrel like other children; her countenance was always tranquil and serene. Whether one caressed her or found fault with her, she was always the same. Her answer was invariably a modest smile, and, though of a warm and lively disposition, she preserved in all the little accidents of childhood, an imperturbable calmness of demeanor. During the entire time that she was with us, we never once had occasion to chastise her. A slight reproof was enough to make her correct the little defects inseparable from that tender age. Two brothers and a sister of hers attended our school with her, and with these she never fell into any fits of childish anger, but invariably gave the best of everything to them. At the common table in the school she was content with what was put before her; and the sweet smile that always lit up her face was an evident expression of her uniform and constant satisfaction.

"Shortly after her entrance into the school, she learned by heart the daily prayers said in the institution, though it took about half an hour to recite them. At five years of age, she read with perfect ease and readiness the Office of the Blessed Virgin and the Office of the Dead, so great was the zeal with which from her earliest years she applied herself to prayer."

Indeed this irresistible attraction for prayer and for the things of the soul constituted the most remarkable trait in the character of Gemma. Her life, when compared to that of other Christian saints, offers at this time no indications of those remarkable occurrences which she experienced in later years. But it does present a striking contrast to the life nowadays led by many Christians. It was essentially supernatural, whilst ours often is frivolous and dissipated by an excessive love of worldly comforts and pleasures. To be pleasing to God, to walk in the ways of the Lord was congenital to Gemma, for to her the things of the soul belonged as much to the essence of life as to eat, play, and sleep. This entirely Pauline conception of Christianity, as an elevation of man to the brotherhood of Christ, making him a living member or limb of His mystical body, has lost much of the reality it once possessed among the Catholics of an older generation. We suffer yet from the material and worldly ideology of the Reformation.

It is said of Gemma that even thus early, she kept away from the little amusements of playmates in order to seek in solitude an opportunity for intimate union of her soul with angels and saints. Once, when four years of age, she was staying at her paternal grandmother's house. There a small cot always stood ready in the good lady's room. It was set aside for Gemma. One day, as it happened, they were all looking for her everywhere. She could not be found in the big house. The grandmother and the uncle, an army officer, were beginning to feel a little nervous when, on casually entering one of the rooms, they saw the child kneeling before an image of the Immaculate Heart of Mary, with rosy face, sweet luminous eyes, and tiny little hands joined in prayer and adoration.

"What a picture for Raphael! I wish I had my camera," the uncle remarked.

"Gemma," cried the grandmother after a moment's silent admiration, "I have been looking for you all over the place."

"Yes, grandmamma, I was saying a Hail Mary to our Blessed Lady. She is so good and beautiful."

It was Gemma's mother, however, who more than anybody else, understood her daughter and noted from the first how divine grace was working in the soul of the little child. Between them existed a kind of spiritual kinship, a close understanding sympathy which is rather felt as an atmosphere than expressed in words. Hence, too, its influence is all the more subtle and penetrating in the formation of character. Compared with this affection of the mother, Signor Enrico's love for his dear little one was less deep and altogether unprophetic. It never found access to the innermost fibers of the heart. He failed to divine the future greatness of his daughter and did not therefore guide her steps toward its attainment.

Aurelia Galgani's character was undoubtedly of a more spiritual type. Though burdened with the care of a large family, she spent much time in prayer, and every morning approached the Holy Table with senti-

ments of lively devotion, even though her failing health made it difficult for her to do so. Soon she became the teacher and directress of
her daughter in the things of God. Often she would call her apart, and
explain to her the mysteries of our Holy Faith lingering with a kind of
instinctive presentiment on some of the touching scenes of the Passion
and on the love Jesus had for her. Suddenly, pointing to the image of Jesus Crucified, she would exclaim: "See this adorable Jesus dead upon the
Cross for us." Words such as these sank deep into the impressionable
heart of the child, who, after listening for quite a long time, would often
pull at her mother's skirt, and say:

"Mamma, tell me some more about Jesus."

At times, the good mother would tell her more, winding up with a short
story of the Madonna so dear to the heart of Italian children. One day
she said to Gemma:

"If I could take you with me to where Jesus calls me, would you come?"

"And where is that?" the child inquired.

"To Paradise, with Jesus and the Angels," replied the mother.

The heart of Gemma filled with joy, and she felt an ardent desire to be
in Paradise, in the company of Jesus and the Angels. In after years she
told her director that she had never lost that desire to be with God in
Paradise which was aroused within her at this tender age.

Signora Galgani was in the habit of preparing her children for first confession with the greatest care as they in turn reached the age of reason.
Every Saturday she took them to the church for confession. When the
time came to do so for Gemma also, she was greatly struck with the
child's extreme accuracy in remembering the smallest faults. Indeed, she
could scarcely refrain from tears at the sight of the seriousness and the
sorrow with which her little one approached the Sacred Tribunal for the
first time. In these ways Aurelia strove to cultivate the tender buds of
virtue of which Gemma gave unmistakable signs. And who can tell how

far a mother's piety aided to determine the sanctity of the daughter? Long afterwards the latter declared that to her mother chiefly did she owe her knowledge of God, her love of prayer and of Jesus Crucified.

But already the black shadow of death was beginning to fall upon Aurelia Galgani. For the last five years the pious lady had been suffering from consumption, a disease which slowly but relentlessly was consuming her day by day. Soon she realized she had to make the great sacrifice of having her children removed from her side altogether. In fact, owing to the nature of the malady, the doctors strictly forbade their presence in the sickroom. Knowing that the end could not be far, she wished Gemma to be admitted to the Sacrament of Confirmation. Carefully she prepared her for it, and called in also the "Mistresses of Christian Doctrine," who came to the house every evening to finish and complete the work she had done during the daytime.

Accordingly, when scarcely seven years old, on May 26, 1885, the child was confirmed by Archbishop Ghilardi in the Basilica of St. Michael in Foro. The church is famous for its marvelous facade rising high above the main body of the edifice, for its tall tower, and for its numerous paintings dating from the best period of Florentine art. At the end of the sacred ceremony the persons who accompanied Gemma wished to remain in the church to hear another Mass by way of thanksgiving. The saintly child was happy to be allowed to stay on and to pray for her sick mother. What then took place we give in her own words.

"Suddenly," she writes, "as I was hearing Mass as well as I could, and praying for mother, I heard a voice in my heart saying: 'Will you give Me your mamma?' 'Yes,' I replied, 'but take me, too.' 'No,' the voice added, 'give Me your mamma without reserve: for the present you must remain with your father. I will take your mother from you to heaven.' I was obliged to say, 'Yes,' and I ran home as soon as Mass was over. My God! I looked at mamma and wept, and could not speak a word."

It was the first locution, the first of those heavenly voices which were to play such an important role in the life of this Virgin Maid of Lucca.

Aurelia Galgani lingered on for some time yet. The beloved child succeeded in obtaining permission to remain at her bedside and often stood there the long hours of the day looking, sobbing, and praying. As the end came nearer and nearer Signor Enrico, for fear of possible infection, was obliged to take a final step. He determined to send Gemma to her Aunt Elena Landi at San Gennaro. There, away from the home in which alone lived her heart, on September 17, 1886, she received the sorrowful news that her mother was no more.

We may well imagine what that meant to the sensitive child just seven years old. Soon she realized that she had no one now to "tell her about Jesus," to take her to church and to confession. Many, before they reach maturity, never know what it means to lose a mother. They grow up from childhood without ever coming into contact with the hard reality of death. This girl found herself face to face with the mystery of death long before she had begun to know the joy of life. Yet she gave the most wonderful example of perfect resignation to the Will of God.

The last words of Aurelia Galgani were: "I freely offer my life to God to obtain the grace of seeing again and rejoicing with my children in heaven."

Chapter III

GIVE ME JESUS

Toward Christmas of 1886, the year in which Gemma's mother died, Signor Enrico decided to recall his children, scattered here and there for precautionary measures at the time of his wife's last sickness, and reunite them once more under the paternal roof.

Elena Landi, with whom Gemma had been staying, was anxious to keep her permanently on account of her exceptional character and attractive manners. But the child's father could not bear to be severed from his beloved one, and insisted on her returning home as soon as possible. The distance from San Gennaro to town was not great and Gemma, having said good-by to her aunt, decided to make it on foot.

It was a frosty winter day. There were no flowers in the grass. The birds had long ago flown away from the trees that on either side of the road stretched forth their bare, leafless branches white with snow. The child's heart, too, was heavy, for she thought of her home bereaved of its tutelary angel, whose vacant place could not be filled again. Signor Enrico had come to meet her at the door and she flew into his arms and allowed him to kiss and embrace her on that day. Yet, Gemma soon resumed her calmness and, in course of time, even put new courage into the souls of all the others.

"Why weep?" she used to say. "Our mamma has gone to heaven. She now suffers no more, while before she suffered so much."

Shortly after her return home, the child was sent as a day scholar to the Sisters of St. Zita, also called Oblates of the Holy Ghost, who ran a boarding and day school in Lucca. She was affectionately received by the Foundress herself, Sister Elena Guerra, one of the band of noble women who have left an ineffaceable record in the history of human events.

Sister Elena was a scholar and, what is immeasurably more, she is now a candidate for Beatification. Like all saints, this great woman had but one purpose in life, one idea. It was the dedication of herself and of all her energies to the task of spreading the devotion to the Holy Ghost. In her way of thinking there could be no other means by which to enkindle the smoldering faith of the people. Just as the work of Redemption belongs to Christ, so to the Holy Ghost belongs that of the sanctification of souls, which He came down to accomplish in the Church on the day of Pentecost. Yet, compared to the Savior, the Third Person of the Blessed Trinity had not, hitherto, entered into the full inheritance of homage due to His divine nature and mission.

Sister Elena Guerra's mind was simple and unsophisticated. In her writings, which attracted some attention, she avoids mere intellectual discussions, but dwells at length on the emotional and practical aspect of the devotion to the Holy Ghost. Christians had not wholly shaken off the legacy of that indifference toward the Holy Ghost which St. Paul had found among the Ephesians. Outside the relatively narrow sphere of mystics and saints, He was little known and not half sufficiently loved by them. She wished Him to be a living reality in their daily prayers and devotions, an ever present

> *Consolator optimus,*
> *Dulcis hospes animae.*
> "Consoler, kindest, best;
> Our bosom's dearest guest."

It was mainly through the exertions of this heroic woman that Pope Leo XIII, by various enactments and especially by his Encyclical Letter, *Divinum Illud Munus*, strove to promote in the Church a deeper knowledge and love of the Holy Ghost.

The following anecdote is full of charm. One day Sister Elena was explaining to some First Communion children the meaning and practice of Spiritual Communion. One of them suddenly asked: "Mother, can we make spiritual confirmation?" "O yes," replied Sister Elena beaming with joy, "each time we say 'Come Holy Ghost' we make a Spiritual Confirmation."

Gemma experienced a wonderful happiness in the new life at St. Zita's. "I began," she says in her autobiography, "to go to school with the nuns. It was like living in Paradise."[6]

She was now nine years old and passionately longed to receive her First Communion. Every day, with tears in her eyes, she begged her teacher or her father or her confessor to let her enjoy the privilege of receiving Jesus in the Holy Sacrament. But there were difficulties in the way, which could not be easily explained to a child, and so her ardent requests were put off by telling her that she should have no faults, no, not even the slightest venial sin. Gemma was fully convinced of the purity of conscience needed to receive her Lord in the Blessed Sacrament. "Give me Jesus," she would say, "and you shall see how good I will be. I shall be quite changed. Give Him to me. I cannot live without Him."

They alone, who have had experience in the sacred ministry of souls, are able to appreciate the advantages a child can derive from the early Eucharistic union with its Lord. The Church, in these latter times, has wisely revived the ancient beautiful custom of the Communion of children.

"We must see the Pope, eh?" said Guy de Fontgalland, when his parents promised him a voyage to Rome, "then I shall say to him: 'Holy Father, I love you because you have told children to make their Communion at seven.'" That was about the year 1920, but in Gemma's days the age of

First Communion was much later, and her family was opposed to any innovation in the accepted traditions.

At her earnest request, however, and through the entreaties of her confessor, Monsignor Giovanni Volpi, afterwards Bishop of Arezzo, who understood the child's heart, she was at length allowed to prepare for the great event. What a happy day it was to be. Children feel an intimate attraction toward Jesus in the Eucharist. It is the blending of divine sanctity with human innocence, and the prelude of that Communion of thought and love which constitutes in heaven the joy of the Blessed. For Gemma it meant so much. She could truly say with the Psalmist: "As the hart panteth after the fountains of water; so my soul panteth after Thee, O God."[7] The First Communion has been the turning point in the life's history of many a Christian soul. In her circumstances, as in those of St. Aloysius and later on of Guy de Fontgalland it altered its outlook and stimulated new hopes. She had learned from her saintly mother that to receive Jesus for the first time was the supreme action of one's life, in preparation for which many prayers and acts of virtue were necessary. Yes, she would welcome the Lord Jesus and make Him an offering of rich gifts, of fruits and flowers nurtured in the fair bower she had built for Him in her soul. There was to be the lily because it spoke to her of purity, and the rose because it spoke of love, and the violet because it spoke of the flower of humility.

To achieve her object the better, she asked and obtained her father's consent to remain ten whole days with the nuns. That would render her more worthy of Jesus in the great Sacrament of Sacraments. Gemma never went home during this time, she saw no one and never stirred from the Convent's gate, spending most of the day in the little chapel of the nuns. But she wrote occasional letters to her father in one of which, speaking of her new life in the Convent, she says: "How happy I am, what a Paradise, what a Paradise!" On the 16th of June Signor Enrico received the following note:

Caro babbo,

It is the eve of my First Communion. Tomorrow will be a day of supreme joy for me. I send you these few lines just to assure you of my great love. I also want to ask you to pray for me so that Jesus, when coming tomorrow for the first time into my heart, may find it less unworthy to receive Him and to receive the graces He has set aside for me. Do forgive me for my many faults, for my disobedience and want of love. This evening you must forget all and send me a big blessing.

Your loving child,
Gemma

That evening one of the Sisters surprised her while intent in jotting down a few resolutions of her future conduct. They read as follows: "(1) I shall go to Confession and receive Holy Communion each time as if it were the last; (2) I shall frequently visit Jesus in the Blessed Sacrament, but more frequently when I am in trouble; (3) I shall do some act of mortification on the eve of every feast of our Lady, and shall always ask her blessing before going to bed; (4) I shall live constantly in the presence of God; (5) when the clock strikes the hour I shall say: 'Have mercy on me, Jesus!' "[8]

The longed-for day dawned at last. No one can express the feelings of this child of nine years better than she herself has done:

"That Sunday morning I rose early and ran to church to receive Jesus for the first time. Finally all my longings were to be gratified. Then I understood the promise of Jesus, 'He who eats of Me, shall live by Me.' It is impossible to describe what passed between Jesus and myself at that moment, it was inexpressible. Jesus made His presence felt intensely, very intensely in my poor soul. I realized then how different are the delights of heaven from those of earth. I was seized by a desire to make that union with God perpetual. I felt myself more detached from the world and more drawn to the things of God."[9]

This does not read like the language of a girl, represented by her biographers as shy and reserved in conversation. It is more akin to the silent speech of the seraphs who stand adoring at the foot of the throne of the Almighty, or to the accents of a mystic whose lips had been touched by the fire of heaven.

For the vast majority of children the First Communion day, like any other day, rises and sets within the appointed span of each season. Its glow and enthusiasm, even the sense of inward gladness experienced by the child, will seldom last beyond the brilliancy of that day's sun. Indeed, such feelings often spring from the feast of love, of light and flowers with which Catholic tradition has surrounded the First Communion day. Yet, in spite of our unconquerable weakness, the memory of the First Communion will not easily be forgotten. It is said of Napoleon that on being asked which was the best day of his life, he unhesitatingly answered: "The day of my First Communion." Possibly this is but one of the many pious aphorisms with which human kindness has endeavored to lighten the gloom cast by history around the great emperor's figure: or is it Napoleon's afterthought, born of the deeper intuition into the vanity of created things, which had purified his soul during the sorrows and humiliation of St. Helena? At any event it expresses the yearning of us all never to forget the glories we have known on the day of our First Communion, for the Eucharist is the center of Catholic intellectual life as well as the basis of Catholic moral and religious conduct.

For Gemma, too, the day of the First Communion swiftly passed away, but its message, the atmosphere of holiness it created around her soul, could no longer be effaced. Henceforward all her Communions were to be like the first. She would never allow them to become a mere matter of routine. There was something Aloysian in her resolution to make a long preparation before, and a long thanksgiving after each new Communion. Jesus in the Holy Eucharist became, in fact, her inseparable companion, the love of her heart. To be more frequently near Him, she would seek the company of her mistresses with whom it was easier to speak of holy things during the hours of recreation. In a special manner

June 17, the anniversary of her First Communion, was to be kept as her spiritual birthday. She often referred to the return of this day when writing to her spiritual Father.

"I am not sure," she says in one of her letters, "if you know the Feast of the Sacred Heart of Jesus is also my feast day. Yesterday was verily a heavenly day. I stayed with Jesus, talked with Jesus, was happy with Jesus and wept with Him. Interior recollection held me more closely united to Jesus than usual. O worldly thoughts go far from me! I want to stay with Jesus and with Him alone. My Jesus, you still bear with me. The more I think of my unworthiness the more am I lost in astonishment, and nothing can calm me until I fly to Your immense mercy, O most merciful Jesus! Where have my thoughts carried me? To the blessed day of my First Communion. Yesterday, the Feast of the Sacred Heart, I experienced again the joy of that happy day of my First Communion. Yesterday, I tasted anew of Paradise. But what is the taste of one day only when we are to enjoy it everlastingly? The day of my First Communion, I can say it with truth, was the day in which I felt my heart most inflamed with love for Jesus. How happy I was when with Jesus in my heart I could exclaim: 'Your Heart, O my God, Your heart is mine. Your beatitude is likewise mine.' " [10]

Chapter IV

SCHOOL DAYS

We would fain dwell long on the school years of Gemma, all the more so because they were short and few. Taking her whole life into consideration it may be said that she was not one of those "sheltered flowers" which have adorned the Church in recent years. Unlike many of them her path lay through fire and water, and she had "a baptism wherein to be baptized." But that was later. The present were the most happy and radiant years of her brief pilgrimage on earth, when the practice of virtue had not as yet brought with it the pain of sacrifice, but only the reward and joy of love. Like a lily of the field, she basked in the sunshine of youth, dear to God and man. No matter what her little task might be, at home or in the Convent, with her it was always May, for the world was young and sweet and good, the yoke of the Lord easy and His burden light. Her father could not for a single day be separated from her, while at St. Zita's she was beloved alike by her mistresses and schoolmates. "You are good, Gemma," Sister Camilla Vagliensi used to say, "and God loves you dearly."

It was this saintly Sister who had initiated her into the ways of meditating on the Passion of our Lord. She seemed to have divined that sorrow and adversity lay in store for the child entrusted to her keeping. "Gemma," she would say, betraying vague yearnings and unresolved doubts in eyes and voice, "I wish you would stay always with us."

"Gemma," wrote one of her mistresses, "was the life of the school and nothing was done without her. All the pupils longed to have her with them at their games, at their little festivities, indeed at everything they did, notwithstanding the fact that she was of a somewhat shy and reserved nature, not given to much speaking, tenacious and resolute, and on occasion, almost brusque and seemingly wanting in courtesy. But no matter what happened, she always had a sweet, gracious smile for everybody, and if she was sparing in words, it was not for want of affection and politeness, but from fear of offending God."

Little girls between the age of six and twelve, especially in Convent schools, are very much alike in dress, features, and behavior. The Sisters are fond of calling them "dear angels," although angels are not supposed to be as full of fun and mischief as most of these girls certainly are. Yet, notwithstanding their ready-made angelic reputation, children are children all the world over. We would not go so far as to say that the little ones at St. Zita's had the faintest notion of purposely avoiding blame at the expense of a friend or a comrade. The Sisters were convinced that they were, one and all, honesty itself in accepting responsibility for their own misdeeds. Perhaps it was so ordinarily. But then that kind of mischief did occur at times and often enough Gemma became the scapegoat or victim of faults she had never committed. Usually she held her peace and cheerfully submitted to the punishment that followed.

"Why don't you speak out?" one of the Sisters, who understood her better, would say.

"Oh, well, never mind, Sister, I didn't think it worthwhile to make a fuss about it."

Sometimes, however, the trick would leak out; it usually does among girls, and then Gemma, on being asked, did not hesitate to tell the truth. For with her, "yes" was "yes," and "no" was "no." Hers was the speech of the gospel, nor would she consent to depart one jot or one tittle from it for the sake of reputation or gain.

We have the assurance of Gemma's spiritual director, that she never committed a deliberate sin, mortal or venial. Faults of frailty, failings due to oversight or immature deliberation she certainly had. They were exceedingly few, and quickly repented of when pointed out to her. They did not escape the notice of her mistresses and companions. Even to her friends she rarely revealed her feelings, and when questioned she would answer with the fewest words possible. She was perhaps too serious for her age, shy and reserved. At times she gave the impression of being cold, and stiff, and proud, chiefly to those who did not know her intimately.

It is in fact through the light which these traits throw upon her character, that we gain an insight into her remarkable virtues. As one reads the lengthy folio pages of witnesses, cited in the processes that led to her canonization, one is made to realize that the charm of her spiritual life, the undisturbed possession of holiness in later years, was not merely a gratuitous gift. She was not, so to say, a born saint, but one in whom nature, will, grace, and education had marvelously combined to develop the initial marks of character in the direction of sanctity. From the first she had a strong determination to turn to good account the gifts she received from on high.

In her spiritual resolutions she writes that henceforth she must keep strict watch over the senses and avoid diligently anything tending to distract her heart from God and the things that belong to Him. The struggle to do this was necessarily hard for flesh and blood. Even such men as Francis of Sales, Ignatius Loyola, and the Seraphic Saint of Assisi were not granted from the start a perfect realization of ideal saintliness. Only by a gradual process of spiritual rebirth did they appear to us in the evening of life, so divinely Christlike, such close images, though ever still imperfect, of the God-made-man. For them, as for Gemma, the reconciliation between the higher and lower aspirations of the self, between the mutually hostile promptings of nature and grace, were the outcome of a slow but continuous process of becoming. It is this that renders the first steps in spiritual life painful and uncertain; that makes the pursuit of sanctity harsh and unattractive in the novice.

"Gemma," Sister Vagliensi used to say, "if I did not read into your eyes, if I did not know you well, I too would think like the others, and call you proud."

In reality the child had no notion of what pride was. The first occasion on which the remark left a conscious impression in her mind was when her attention was called to the sin of pride by the Superior of the school. She had warned Gemma to be on her guard against this fault owing to the report of some Sisters as yet unacquainted with the child's character.[11]

Walking home from the school in the evening Gemma ran to her aunt and said: "The Superior told me that I have given way to pride today. How can I have been proud? Do, please, explain to me what I must do to avoid being proud, for, really, I don't know this kind of sin."

"Ask the Superior to explain it to you," answered her aunt. Gemma obeyed. After the explanation was given, she said:

"Mother, I am stupid, but have I really been proud?"

Indeed, Gemma was not proud. Though of a naturally vivacious temperament, as one of her teachers thought, she nevertheless seemed always very quiet. On no occasion did she allow her temper to gain the upper hand, and when some of her companions contended with her or abused her, as children often do among themselves, the invariable answer was a friendly glance followed by such a sweet smile, that the would-be adversary could only throw her arms around her neck and embrace her affectionately.

It is impossible to exaggerate the part played by prayer in Gemma's spiritual development. Even thus early it had become the sole anchor and refuge of her life, the cornerstone upon which she would raise the supernatural edifice in future years. It was a standing joke among the girls when any Sister asked the whereabouts of Gemma, to answer: "Sister, she is in the chapel." And there she frequently was, kneeling before the Blessed Sacrament, with large soft eyes fixed on the little golden door that held her Jesus. It was Victor Hugo who said that morning and evening prayers are the "toilet of the soul." Those who neglect them become careless of venial sin. Gemma had learned from her saintly mother never to omit this supernatural toilet; she also learned from the Sisters to add a short meditation on the Passion and a five minutes' examination of conscience in the evening. In fact piety was her most conspicuous virtue. Under the cooling and life-giving power of this heavenly dew she blossomed, like a rose of grace, in deeds and prayers rather than words.

Referring to her habit of intimate union with God, Sister Giulia Sestini, who succeeded Sister Vagliensi, both in affection and admiration for Gemma, says:

"By reason of my office I had to be with this saintly girl more than the other Sisters and was constantly struck by her piety and childlike candor. From the very first days I knew her, I felt she was a soul very near to God, though hidden from the world. I noticed later, when I was urging the children to the practice of mental prayer in the morning and examination of conscience in the evening, that she, who was already advanced in these things, took the instruction more to heart than her companions. But Gemma never told me how much time she gave to prayer, and only from a few short answers, when questioned on the subject, did I learn that she really devoted a great deal of time to meditation."

Every evening, on coming home from school, she shut herself up in her little room and said the whole rosary on her knees; also several times during the night she rose and for about a quarter of an hour would commend her soul and its needs to Jesus. Every morning she went to hear Mass with her aunts in the beautiful church of St. Michael, and from the year 1890 on began to receive Holy Communion every day. "Jesus," she writes in one of her many letters, "made His presence felt in my poor soul, more and more. He said much to me and gave me very great consolation." Such and similar expressions are met with in almost every page of her correspondence with the confessor and spiritual director. They testify to that habitual union with God, to that love of Jesus in the Blessed Sacrament which constitutes the characteristic of Gemma's sanctity.

But whilst thus intent upon God, Gemma by no means neglected her studies; indeed this child of Christ was one of the most diligent of pupils, carrying off quite a number of prizes at the annual examinations. In the school year 1893-94, she won the gold medal for religious knowledge. Often at the yearly distribution of prizes, too, her mistresses contrived, despite her natural humility, to exhibit some of her compositions, verses, and French exercises. So keen was she upon study that frequently at home they remarked to her: "Why are you always at your books, Gemma? You know more than enough for your age and yet you never seem to be satisfied."

On some special occasions they had little plays at the Convent. Gemma was pretty, had a love for music, a good voice, and a pleasing way of delivering. She would naturally be asked to take a part in the performance which, to please the Sisters, she never failed to do. One day, while the children were having a rehearsal, the Mother Superior entered the room, and asked Sister Giulia to make the children pray for a certain person, a friend of the Convent, who was on his deathbed and had refused to receive the Sacraments of the Church. They all knelt and prayed, and when they resumed the play, Gemma came near the mistress and said in a whisper: "Sister, the grace is granted." True enough, the news reached them in the course of the evening that the gentleman, for whom they had prayed, had died a peaceful and holy death.

"Come on, children," one day the lively Sister Giulia said to her pupils, "let us have a bit of fun. We will draw lots to find out who among you shall be a saint."

Well, the lots were drawn amidst shouts of joy and peals of laughter, and, explain it as you will, the lot on that day fell upon Gemma, whose only comment upon the incident was to smile one of her sweet smiles saying:

"Yes, I shall become a saint."[12]

Chapter V

IN SIGHT OF CALVARY

In 1894 Gemma, now in the sixteenth year of her age, was a happy girl, the idol of the family and a paragon of virtue for all who knew her. Almost daily on returning from school she would accompany her father in his walks to the fortification, or further out into the open country outside the gates of the city. On such occasions, shyly and tentatively, she would disclose to him some of her intimate secrets and speak of inner voices that were urging her to an intenser love of the Crucified Savior. Signor Enrico, who had set his heart on a university career for this child, listened, wondered, and was perplexed. But he laid all these things up in his heart and would say to himself: "What an one, think ye, shall this child be?"[13]

On their way back oftentimes a pale yellow glow deepened behind the mountains, and church bells from afar rang the Angelus. The two stopped to pray whilst the bells rang and they recalled to her mind the mystery of Christ's Incarnation.

In the house she was the teacher of her little sisters and the angel of her brothers, to whom she devoted herself with great affection. It was a life not without thorns, but the following expression of her elder brother tells its own story: "Gemma always brings the olive branch."[14] Indeed the sweetness of her character endeared her not only to those of the household but to friends also who came to visit the family.

It happened one day that her godmother at Confirmation made her a present of a gold watch with golden chain and cross. Gemma, as any other girl would, was delighted with the gift and on the first occasion, partly for the mere pleasure of it and partly to please the donor, wore it in going out of the house. On her return she seemed to hear the voice of her angel who said:

"The jewels of the bride of Christ are not made of gold but of thorns and splinters from the wood of the cross."

This is the first record we possess of angelic voices and apparitions which were later to become so common in the life of our Saint. She, of course, at once laid the watch aside promising our Lord never again to adorn her person with the trinkets of vanity. From that moment Gemma's love for Jesus Crucified which, as we stated above, forms the distinctive characteristic of her sanctity, increased a hundredfold.

"I wish to suffer," she used to repeat with St. Mary Magdalen de Pazzi, "I wish to suffer much for Jesus," and then she renewed her determination to become a saint. It was at this time that she chose Bartolomea Capitanio, recently raised to the honor of the altars, as her model. She well knew that to become a saint one must live and die on the cross for, though pain is not of the essence of holiness, it is nonetheless for us, children of a fallen race, one of its necessary conditions.

Among her brothers and sisters. Gemma's heart clung with a kind of preferential love to Gino. He was a youth of a singularly sweet and gentle disposition. Though some two years her senior — he was born on June 5, 1876 — he not only admired but strove to copy the virtues of his younger sister. There was deep understanding sympathy between them arising from the similarity of aims and aspirations and from those forebodings of an early doom that hung over them. Gino had inherited the malady of his mother. He was eighteen years of age, was studying for the priesthood, and had already received the Minor Orders, when he was stricken with a sudden attack of consumption. He died in September, 1894. The loving sister, unmindful of the risk to herself, had remained day and night by his bedside throughout his sickness.

"I suffered much," she wrote afterwards, "but was fully resigned to the will of God." Once before, at the death of her mother, she had uttered this cry of resignation. Today she utters it again. "Not my will, but God's, be done." It is in such outpourings of the heart scattered through the autobiography, and bursting forth at every crisis of her sorrowful story, that we catch glimpses of Gemma's heroic character.

As we look at her stepping into girlhood we seem to discern in the calm and perfectly symmetrical features of her countenance, hidden traces of that strong determination to seek and to see God in all things. It has been said of a great woman of the world, Sarah Bernhardt, that she never obeyed anybody or anything except her own imperious will. Men may well admire such strength of will power in a woman, but so long as this does not rise above the natural level it is doomed to sterility. It leaves the human heart exactly as it was at the suit, because it takes for granted its absolute perfection and substitutes the self for God. By a simpler process of supernatural intuition Gemma realized that the perfection of our will consists in a complete surrender to the Will of its Maker manifested through the various accidents of creation. To be no more than a tool in God's hands, that is what Gemma aspired to be.

In childhood, her moral features, like the lineaments of her face, appeared vague and undefined. They had now grown and were still to develop in character and definition during the few years that were to remain to her. Pious she had been and innocent from early years, but real sanctity, as men understand it, was to be reared at the foot of the cross. We shall meet her in the thick of sorrows and temptations, an object of pity, and alternately of veneration and of scorn, but living always "in the great Taskmaster's eye," and perfectly resigned to His Will.

The death of Gino brought sorrow to the Galgani family. It perhaps marked the beginning of Gemma's long series of trials. Either owing to the fatigue during the days of her brother's illness, or because of her

grief at his loss, she soon fell dangerously ill and had to remain in bed
for nearly three months. After recovering she remained so weak and
exhausted that the doctor advised her withdrawal from school. We can
well imagine the pain she endured at the separation from the beloved
Convent. It had been her second home for many years, and the Sisters at
St. Zita's had been like so many mothers to her. But Divine Providence
pointed in a new direction and Gemma willingly retired into the solitude
of her family. Day by day she regained strength, to the great joy of her
father, but to Gemma the return of health brought no special joy or
consolation.

"From the moment," she writes, "that mother inspired me with the
desire of Heaven, I have never ceased to long for it, and had the choice
been left to me, I would have preferred to die and go to my God. In
sickness I used to experience a fresh sense of pleasure whenever I felt
worse, and a kind of sorrow every time I grew stronger. One day, after
Holy Communion, I asked Jesus why He did not take me to heaven:
'Daughter,' He replied, 'because during your life I shall give you many
occasions of greater merit, redoubling your desire for heaven, and giving
you the grace to support with patience your life upon earth.' "

Gemma now settled down to the quiet round of daily duties in the
home, and did all she could for her little brothers and sisters. It was noticed that her love of prayer grew more intense and she began to spend
many hours every day in intimate converse with our Lord, chiefly when
she received Him in Holy Communion. Jesus revealed Himself to her on
many occasions and was, in fact, her inseparable companion. Her soul,
already prepared by grace, was opening like a flower to the rays of the
Eucharistic Sun eagerly expanding to receive the rich profusion of its
light and warmth.

Christ, we read in the life of St. Catherine of Siena, used, at times
visibly, to accompany this Saint, as on the day when walking to and fro
and reciting her breviary in front of the chapel, she became aware of
someone walking by her side. It was Jesus. The virgin continued to recite

the Latin words of the psalm with deepest devotion. At the conclusion of it, on reaching the doxology of Pope Damasus, she slightly modified the words, and turning toward Jesus whispered, trembling with emotion: "Glory be to the Father, 'to Thee,' and to the Holy Ghost."[15] Very similar was Gemma's familiarity with the Divine Savior. She spoke to Him as to a friend or a brother, asking questions and receiving answers, praying to Him, not in the conventional formulas of vocal prayer, but with the intimacy that springs from passionate love.

In these heart-to-heart communings with Jesus, she learned that a new storm was about to break upon her during the year 1895.

"What will befall me this year," she writes, "I know not. I abandon myself to You, O God. All my hopes and affections shall be for You. I am weak, my Jesus, but I trust in Your strength, and resolve to live closer and closer to You."

In fact she soon fell into one of those mysterious maladies which from henceforward will never leave her. This time the sickness was declared to be necrosis of the foot. She tried to bear the pain in silence, but owing to an accidental fall of a heavy plank, the foot became so inflamed that an operation was found absolutely necessary. A surgeon was called in, who, as soon as he saw the foot, was filled with alarm and expressed his fear that amputation would be necessary. Before, however, resorting to this extreme step, he laid open the diseased bone and began to scrape it thoroughly. Desirous of suffering, Gemma refused to take an anesthetic, and with her eyes fixed on her Crucified Lord, without a groan, stood the deep incision of the foot and the painful scraping of the bone. This illness lasted many months. It brought fresh agonies of sorrow to Signor Enrico, and new expenses at a time when he could no longer bear them.

Gemma was not slow to perceive that a change was coming on in the family circumstances. Like most Italian girls she had a great love for the poor. "Whenever I went out," she says in her autobiography, "I asked papa to give me some money, and if, as sometimes was the case, he refused, I had at least bread and clothes to give away. It was God's will I should meet these poor people, and every time I went out I encountered some three or four of them. To those who called at the house I gave clothing or whatever I could lay my hands on, until I was forbidden by the confessor to do so. But a day came when papa gave me no more money, nor was I allowed to take anything from the house, yet every time I went out I seemed to meet none but those in distress. They all ran to me and I had nothing to give. I wept with grief and resolved to go out no more."

Signor Enrico had been carrying on a very successful business as a chemist when, suddenly, his affairs took a bad turn. He had always been liberal, most free in giving away money, and had allowed his daughter to become a mother to the poor. It was a common saying that all he had slipped through his fingers like sand. Himself a perfect pattern of moral integrity in business transactions, he trusted implicitly in the honesty of others. He lent money to various people and unwisely stood security for others. The failure of rents from his lands, the long sickness and death of his wife and two children had greatly reduced his resources. One by one the bills which he had signed fell due and all his property, movable and immovable, was seized by the creditors, so that both he and his family were thrown into utter destitution. Sometime after, he fell ill with cancer of the throat. Gemma, who had just gotten over her own sickness, was constantly by his bedside, animating, consoling, and preparing him to receive the last Sacraments. He died on November 11, 1897, leaving her a penniless orphan.

In the last letter to his Benedictine nieces Henri Bremond wrote: "May we, this year, know how to accept as joyously as possible all that the divine tenderness may cause us to suffer." In a similar, or even greater spirit of resignation. Gemma writes:

"We entered 1897, the most sorrowful year for all the family. I alone unmoved, remained indifferent amidst such misfortunes. At home all were sad and unconsolable both because of daddy's sickness and because of the loss of our property. One morning I fully realized the sacrifice for which Jesus wished us to be soon ready. I wept much in those days, but Jesus was speaking so loudly to my heart and was giving so much patience to my father that I became strong and calmly prepared to receive from Jesus the impending calamity."

At the time of her father's death Gemma was not in the room of her dying parent. The family doctor, Signor Del Prete, went to her and said:

"I have a sad news to give you."

"How is daddy?" inquired Gemma.

"He is gone to heaven," said the doctor.

"Oh, yes," she exclaimed, "now I can be a nun," and trying to compose herself she fell in a swoon. On coming to herself she wiped her tears which she said were unworthy of the bride of the Crucified Lord. Later she wrote in her autobiography:

"Even on the day on which papa died, Jesus forbade me to give way to unnecessary grief, and I spent it in prayer, perfectly resigned to God's most Holy Will. Henceforth He became my earthly and heavenly Father. After papa's death ... we were left absolutely destitute without even the means of supporting life."[16]

Gemma, some of whose writings attain the distinction of literary form, is usually sober and very much matter of fact in the story of her early life. Even in speaking of the death of her father, she does not lay open to us the secret feelings of her heart. He was only fifty-seven when he died, and left behind him three sons and three daughters, penniless and orphaned. But a scene occurred which even Gemma could never forget. Scarcely had her father closed his eyes when the creditors in large numbers rushed in upon the little group to close the pharmacy, to seize what little furniture still remained, and to search even Gemma's own pockets, taking away the few small coins they found in her purse. The scene made such a lasting and painful impression upon her mind that, during the mental agonies and wanderings of her last illness, she saw over again these pitiless oppressors of the poor searching her home, and laying hands on all they could find, regardless of the death that was within those walls.

Chapter VI

THE MIRACULOUS CURE

The Galgani family was now reduced to the extreme of indigence and destitution. They had to depend on their relatives for the means of subsistence and oftener than not even for their daily bread. To one of a character different from Gemma's own this sudden fall of the family into utter poverty, at an age when she most needed the help of its reputation and support, might well have been a source of discouragement. Was this the reward of her virtues, her prayers and Communions? But Gemma had trained herself to see in all things the Divine Will, and courageously faced the future trusting in God's Providence that was to her "an anchor of the soul sure and firm." Nor did she trust in the kindness of Providence in vain. Carolina Lencioni, an aunt in easy circumstances, invited Gemma to reside with her in Camaiore, a village not far from Lucca. So timely an offer could hardly be refused without causing offense. It both relieved the distress of the family and provided a comfortable home for our Saint.

This arrangement, having been agreed upon, Gemma settled quietly in the new house, bringing to it the sunshine that accompanied her everywhere. But Jesus, who had chosen this child for Himself, was knocking at the door of her soul filling it with an ever increasing abundance of graces and extraordinary favors. After a short stay at Camaiore, she began to feel that the new surroundings did not suit her temperament and the spiritual aspirations of her soul. For one thing they demanded too much of her time and attention in the way of dressing, visits, and social amusements.

Even in the palmy days of her life at home Gemma had had no share in the constant round of gaiety that fell to the lot of most girls of her age and position — the plays, the flower shows and garden parties, the dancing at fashionable clubs. Mrs. Galgani had not known such things, and would scarcely have approved of them for Gemma. No wonder if this sort of life seemed almost a waste to her. She did not feel as though she belonged to it. It was making her restless. A love episode, of which, all unknowingly, she had become the romantic heroine, decided her to take the final step and to ask her aunt's permission to return home.

At this time Gemma was in her nineteenth year. She dressed plainly, was not tall, nor did she possess that combination of qualities which modern taste would expect in a beautiful girl. Withal she was attractive, had a dignified bearing, delicate complexion, and a graceful gentle manner. Her eyes were large, soft, and luminous. They reflected as in a mirror the interior beauty of the soul. Her smile was fascinating. Sister Gesualda, author of one of the most popular lives of Gemma in Italian, had once had the opportunity to admire her wonderful smile: "One day," she says, "I saw her smile: the charm of it impressed me so much that I have never since forgotten it."

At home, in Lucca, she had been much admired by an Officer who had followed her in her walks and would, no doubt, have made further advances had she not done all in her power to avoid him. It now happened that a young man of a good family, the son of a local doctor, was so attracted by Gemma's unassuming beauty and her quiet feminine ways, that he fell deeply in love with her. As is usual with most young men of this class he avowed to be unhappy without Gemma and already dreamed dreams of a world stirred by the south wind, and the breath of flowers, and the birds that chirp in the trees. He must needs speak of these new hopes to his father and of his proposed marriage. At first nothing seemed easier to the good doctor. He would speak to the relatives of the girl. He knew them and was sure that in the circumstances they could have no objections to the proposed arrangements. He, therefore, on behalf of his son, asked Gemma's uncle for the honor of her hand. It all seemed so providential. From a human standpoint the union of these two souls was all but natural and most desirable. It meant so much for Gemma and for her brothers and sisters. But, although she had as yet no definite idea of the future which lay before her, there was that in her soul which bade her keep her freedom. She was already thinking of the convent and of its life wholly dedicated to Jesus Christ in virginal chastity. Even from childhood her world had stretched beyond the earth into the realm of religious mysteries; the call of the spirit had drawn her insistently apart amidst the ordinary pleasures of her younger years. When therefore her aunt, the Signora Lencioni, spoke of the proposed marriage and, with a motherly interest, endeavored to show its many advantages Gemma had but one answer to give. She wished to belong to Jesus alone; she was grateful to her aunt and to the young man for the proposal, but she did not intend to marry.

Here we must pause and reflect. No doubt worldly wisdom will smile significantly at this unexpected turn of the affair and at this waste of a golden opportunity. Let us not quarrel with those who would fain think in that way.

Marriage is a Sacrament of divine institution, necessary in ordinary circumstances to the individual, and necessary to the race of which he is a unit. The marriage promise comes at a moment of tremendous import in the life of a maiden just stepping from girlhood onto the threshold of prospective motherhood. Born to love more intensely than man, she feels a strong impulse to blend her exuberant life with the life of another, and pour therein the treasures of her heart. In this dedication, capable of sublime sacrifices, lies the happiness of a woman's existence. The world possesses all the magic that excites this feminine tendency. Indeed all the power and grandeur of the world should reverently bow at the passage of a girl advancing to the altar to consecrate the sunshine and poetry of her life irrevocably to her husband and to God. Yet, let us also reverently bow before the mystery hidden in the soul of a young girl when she hears the sound of the divine voice. What would the world come to without the sacrifice, the prayers, and the purity of these even nobler beings?

To return to the narrative. In order to avoid further trouble Gemma's aunt, not without genuine regret, permitted her to return to Lucca. She even gave her a little wardrobe for the day of her admission into the convent. It was, however, to a home of poverty and destitution where everything was wanting that Gemma directed her steps.

On the day of his wife's death Signor Enrico had invited two of his sisters, Elisa and Elena Galgani, to stay with him and take care of the children. One of them, known in the autobiography as Aunt Elisa, had been a second mother to Gemma all these years. It is mainly from her sworn depositions in the Processes of Gemma's beatification that we derive the information we possess about our Saint's life at this period. On this occasion, however, Signora Elisa did not extend the usual welcome to her niece. She greeted her coldly and with a look of thinly concealed disappointment. The fact is Signora Elisa had heard of the marriage offer and of her niece's refusal which, in the present circumstances, seemed to her practical mind so preposterous and utterly absurd.

"Gemma," she said, "why do you come back, did they not love you at Camaiore?"

"I was happy there," answered Gemma, "but I do not want to marry; I wish to belong entirely to Jesus."

In reality Aunt Elisa loved her niece dearly but at the moment things were hard for the Galganis. Here is what she wrote about the family's conditions at this period in one of her depositions.

"We were penniless. All our property (even that of the two ladies, Elisa and Elena Galgani) had passed into the hands of Signor Enrico's creditors. For some time we had to live exclusively on the charity of friends and relatives, later on, Gemma's eldest brother, Guido, began to earn money as a chemist and compounder in the town hospital."

"We were so poor," she says elsewhere, "that we lacked even the most necessary things. But Gemma was ever happy and did her best to encourage us in our trials and difficulties. She used to take little or no food, leaving all that was given to her to be shared among her brothers. Often she said to me: 'Trust in Providence, dear aunt, for Providence will never fail us' and, indeed Divine Providence never abandoned us during those days for we always had something to eat at our meals."

Such was the home to which Gemma had returned. With perfect resignation to God's Holy Will she began to busy herself cheerfully in all the duties of the household, spending the whole day and a great part of the night between prayer and domestic work.

But saints are born to suffer and to teach us by their example the unfathomable mystery of the cross. Soon after coming home Gemma was once more afflicted with one of those periodical maladies which seem to form part of her martyrdom during the brief span of her career on earth. At first she tried hard to bear it all in silence, but soon the inflammation of the kidneys took a serious turn and Gemma was forced to confide her troubles to Aunt Elisa who insisted on a medical visit. But how to persuade this timid, simple, and innocent girl to place herself in the hands of a doctor? Writing about it she says: "Since a long time I was feeling pain in that part of my body but never wished to look or touch myself for I had heard in a sermon as a child that our body is the temple of the Holy Ghost. Those words of the preacher left a great impression on me so that as far as I could I kept a most jealous custody of my body. I could not show myself to a doctor. The mere idea of it made me cry."[17]

The sickness, however, was becoming more serious day by day. Soon to the nephritis other ailments were added, such as paralysis, accompanied by deafness and total loss of hair. Gemma had to take to her bed where she lay for over a year, unable to make the least movement without assistance. All that was possible in the straitened circumstances of the family was done in order to obtain a cure, but to no purpose. The poor girl suffered intensely, not so much because of her bodily pains as because of the additional burden entailed on her dear ones. To all this must be added the repeated temptations of the evil spirit who often would whisper to her ears: "Listen to me, I can take away your sickness; I will most assuredly cure you and make you happy."

It was at this time that Gemma, with the consent of her confessor, made a vow of virginity, and for the sake of her family asked God's help, promising to enter religion if He would grant her a speedy recovery. One night the Passionist student, St. Gabriel of the Sorrowful Mother,[18] whose life she had been reading, appeared to her and said: "Gemma, make your vow to be a religious, but add nothing to it." She did not understand what the Saint meant by these words, and asked why she might not. He merely answered: "My sister," and smiled sweetly. He then took the heart which the Passionists wear, gave it to her to kiss, and placed it on her breast outside the coverlet, and repeating again the words, "My sister," disappeared.

Days rolled on and Gemma grew worse. The doctors in a last attempt to save her, determined to cauterize the spine in twelve places. That was on January 4, 1899. As on a previous occasion she refused to take an anesthetic, preferring to remain the guardian of her body rather than accept any alleviation of the pain.

We read in the life of the Seraphic Saint of Assisi that in like circumstances to those of Gemma he did for a moment fear lest in the application of the hot iron he might shrink from the pain: then bracing his spirit for the ordeal he exclaimed: "O my brother fire; amongst all creatures most noble and useful, be courteous to me in this hour, for I have ever loved thee and ever will love thee for love of Him who created thee."[19] Gemma had not the poetry of St. Francis but she had his spirit and the will to suffer for Christ. The serene endurance with which she

underwent all these operations was a marvel to those who attended her.
The cauterizing, however, proved fruitless; her infirmities increased so
much that on February 2 she writes: "I received Holy Communion by
way of Viaticum. I made my confession and expected every moment to
go to Jesus. The doctors, believing I was no longer able to hear them,
said amongst themselves that I should not live till midnight."[20]

A physician who had been called in for special consultation diagnosed
the case as hysteric paralysis of the spine for which, he said, the only
remedy lay in faith cure. It was necessary to find someone in whom
the patient had implicit confidence. Monsignor Volpi, the confessor of
Gemma, seemed the right person to make the attempt both by reason
of his office, and of the high esteem in which he was held by the patient. He was a man of great prudence, learning, and piety, who in 1897
became auxiliary Bishop to Archbishop Ghilardi of Lucca and, shortly
after Gemma's death, Bishop of Arezzo. Leo XIII was wont to call him,
"The saint of Lucca." Monsignor Volpi was Gemma's ordinary confessor to the end of her life. On this occasion he willingly consented to try
the experiment, not indeed because he believed in the statement of the
doctor, but, as he afterwards asserted in the canonical processes, "with
the intention of obtaining a miracle through the intercession of Blessed
Margaret Mary Alacoque," in whose canonization he was much interested. It thus came about that on February 29 the Monsignor paid a visit to
Gemma, found her wholly indifferent to life and death, and, on leaving,
suggested a novena to Blessed Margaret Mary, assuring the sick girl that
she would be perfectly cured before the nine days were over.

Meanwhile other visitors came to see Gemma, attracted by the fame
of her sanctity and heroic patience. The Sisters of St. Zita, by whom
she had been educated, were constantly at her bedside, night and day. It
happened that her old mistress, Sister Giulia Sestini, came to see her and
she too suggested the making of a novena to Blessed Margaret Mary,
assuring Gemma that the Saint would either work a miracle, or obtain
for her a straight passage to heaven.

Gemma consented and began the novena that very evening, but being too ill, forgot all about it on the day following. At her third attempt to resume it, St. Gabriel appeared to her and made her repeat with him nine times the Pater, Ave, and Gloria.

"Would you be cured?" he asked.

"I wish to do the will of God; for me to die or to live is all one," she answered.

"You will recover," he said, and promised he would come every evening to say the prayers with her.

"The last evening but one of the novena arrived," writes Gemma, "and I wanted to receive Holy Communion on the day following which happened to be the First Friday of March. The confessor was sent for, I made my confession and received Holy Communion the next morning. What happy moments I passed with Jesus! He too asked me: 'Gemma, do you wish to be cured?' I was so intensely moved that I could not give any answer but only said in my heart: 'Jesus, Thy will be done; dear Jesus.' The grace was granted; I was cured and after two hours I rose from my bed. Those around me wept for very joy. I was happy also, not so much because of the health that had been restored to me, as for the words He so kindly addressed to me. 'Gemma,' He said, 'I choose you for My daughter. I shall be to you like a father, and she (pointing to our Blessed Lady) shall be your mother.' " [21]

There never was any doubt as to the instantaneous and complete cure of Gemma from the mysterious sickness which had baffled the skill of the doctors. The news of the recovery spread like wild fire throughout Lucca, and many visitors same to see the miraculously cured girl. Was it all the result of autosuggestion? No doubt the physician who had asked Monsignor Volpi to try the effect of the novena, believed so, and many others may even now be of his mind. It is left to each one to see, or not to see, the finger of God in this as well as in many other preternatural events that play such an important part in the spiritual life of the saints, even as they did in the life of this wonderful girl.

To judge her aright, we must bear in mind that at no period of her sickness does she reveal the symptoms of hysteria. She is always calm, and fully resigned to God's will. She is amiable, obedient, wholly happy in bearing the cross for the sake of our Lord. We must not forget also that her life exhibits a continuous endeavor to practice the highest and most sublime virtues of Christian heroism. Finally the fact that the Church has raised Gemma Galgani to the honors of the altar should be sufficient proof, if any be needed, to make us accept God's special intervention, even though the Divine action did not entirely set aside, but rendered possible, the natural play of mental and organic forces reacting upon the external situations. What is essentially needed in a miracle is the presence of divine causality performing what nature would not be able to perform or could not have performed in the given circumstances. This doctrine is true not only of particular divine favors, it is true also of sanctity. Grace sanctifies, empowers, and elevates nature, but neither destroys it, nor transforms it substantially. Thus can we explain the marvelous variety of form and character in the sanctity of great Christian souls, who were actuated by the power and influence of the same grace.

Once again Gemma resumed the round of her household duties as well as her life of incessant prayer. Often Jesus appeared visibly to her and she would fall into an ecstasy of love, remaining for several hours at a time prostrate on the ground in His presence. Sometimes she also had "intellectual visions and locutions," that is, manifestations in which the exterior senses were in no way affected. The things seen and words heard were then impressed upon her mind, and gave her wonderful strength in trials. They also reprimanded her for any unfaithfulness, and consoled her in her many troubles.

These phenomena, which began to recur more frequently after the miraculous cure, will so increase during the years that still remain, as to place Gemma among mystics like St. Teresa of Avila, and St. Mary Magdalen de Pazzi. Unable to reconcile such graces with her shortcomings, which her delicate conscience represented as grievous faults,[22] she had constant recourse to her confessors for spiritual direction. As we shall see in the course of this narrative, the more that she attempted to resist these divine favors, in obedience to her directors, the more powerfully did God work in her soul. The whole city of Lucca was stirred by the reports of the visions and ecstasies of this most humble among its girls.

Chapter VII

KNOCKING AT THE GATES OF THE CONVENT

One unsatisfactory feature in Gemma's long correspondence is that it dispenses with anything like orderly chronological arrangement. The letters both to Father Germano[23] and to her confessor are not dated; record of time must have seemed to her quite superfluous for the purpose at hand. In the published volume the letters are grouped according to subject, and afford but little indication of the time when and the circumstances under which they were written. The difficulty is increased by the fact that the same, or nearly the same, set of ideas runs through almost all her correspondence. In one of these letters,[24] which was probably written during the early months of 1900, she refers to her vocation and tells Father Germano that for a number of years she had had an ardent desire to enter the convent. Indeed within the circle of friends and relatives her vocation had long been a foregone conclusion. She had grown up among them as a being apart, a being with a destiny, whilst other sons and daughters had come, so to say, to fill the rooms under the paternal roof. Some sort of preternatural atmosphere seemed to hover around her. No wonder that the request to be a nun caused no surprise when it came, and met with no opposition. But from the very first Gemma's vocation to the religious life seemed to be wrapped in mystery. In reality she was not destined to die a nun.

Though Gemma's uppermost thought was now to enter the cloister she yet hesitated as to the congregation of nuns to which God was in a special manner calling her. According to the teaching of St. Thomas, each religious order is distinguished by the practice of a virtue of Christ which it chooses to honor in a particular manner. But which virtue did God will her to make her own in order to be well pleasing to Him?

At the time of her last illness she had been visited by the Sisters of St. Camille de' Lellis, a Congregation of nurses better known as "Barbantini," from the name of their Foundress. One day, together with some of them, a girl came who had not as yet been admitted to the Institute because of her extreme youth. Gemma was moved at her sight. It seemed as if the vision of an angel had appeared bidding her take the narrow path that most surely leads to Christ. She turned to the Novice Mistress of the girl, Sister Leonilda, and straightaway obtained a promise of being received into the order on her recovery. On the other hand, the Passionist St. Gabriel had repeatedly called her "sister." Add to this that the strictness of the Rule of this religious congregation provided an additional attraction in a life of penance and prolonged prayer. There were also the Visitation nuns who appealed strongly to her heart. They had a convent in Lucca where Gemma had spent days of unspeakable joy in the company of the Sisters.

In the midst of all these perplexities it was but natural for her to have recourse to her confessor, Monsignor Giovanni Volpi. He had known Gemma since the time of her First Communion; he had great sympathy for her many sorrows and shared the secrets of her beautiful soul. Taking into consideration the delicate state of her health, Monsignor Volpi decided in favor of the Visitation and undertook to recommend her to the Mother Superior for admission to this Institute. The nuns of the Visitation, also called Salesian Sisters, were founded in 1610 at Annecy, in the Duchy of Savoy, by St. Francis de Sales and by St. Jane de Chantal. The aim of their founder was to secure the benefit of the religious life for persons who had neither the physical strength nor the attraction for the corporal austerities at that time general in religious congregations. It is well known that at first St. Francis had not a strict religious order in mind but one without external vows, where the rule of enclosure should be observed only during the year of novitiate, after which the Sisters should be free to go out by turns to visit the sick and the poor. It was Archbishop de Marquemont of Lyons who persuaded the saintly Bishop of Geneva to follow the common practice and erect his congregation into a religious order under the Rule of St. Augustine, with the cloister imposed by the Council of Trent. St. Francis resisted at first but yielded in the end, and in 1616 undertook the compilation of the "Constitutions" *pour les religieuses de la Visitation Sainte-Marie.* The Church has declared that in his religious order the Saint has added to the Rule of St. Augustine "Constitutions which are admirable for wisdom, discretion, and sweetness." The most striking feature of these constitutions is moderation and common sense. For the past three centuries the Visitation has never stood in need of reform and each century has brought to the Church and the world its contingent of holy souls. It is to a nun of the Visitation, St. Margaret Mary Alacoque of Paray-le-Monial, that our Savior appeared in order that the devotion to the Sacred Heart of Jesus might be established and spread in the Church.

On May 1 of this same year, 1899, the day appointed by the Rev. Mother Superior, Gemma eagerly set off for the convent. It was her marriage day; a happy smile lit up her face and shone in her dark eyes, for was she not going to a lover's tryst?

There was to be a retreat of eight days prior to her admission, and she meant to spend them all before the Blessed Sacrament in the closest union with the mystic Bridegroom of her soul. But things do happen in this world that often upset our best calculations and arrangements. Oh, the impenetrable mystery of God's holy Will. When you, good easy man, think how well you stand and how the earth is shaping in obedience to the dreams of your fancy, suddenly God's own designs break in, and point in another direction. It has ever been so in the life of the saints and, for the matter of that, in the life of many a Christian soul. Seldom does the light of heaven shine upon our eyes as it did upon those of Saul on the road to Damascus. It is only after many trials and disappointments that most men come painfully to rest and to find peace in God's adorable Will. *E in la sua voluntade é somma pace.*[25]

The Rule of the Visitation does not prescribe, as we said, such austerities of the cloister as rising at night, sleeping on hard boards, and great corporal penances. Its founder gave to interior mortification that importance which he withdrew from the external austerities. Gemma, moreover, was not strong. For this very reason the Sisters had shown her special kindness. It thus came about that a thought dawned upon her mind suggesting that perhaps the Visitation was not the place to which God called her. An inner voice seemed to indicate a more austere mode of life. In some way the Mother Superior either came to know or divined what was passing in the candidate's heart. In spite of these mental troubles Gemma wished to stay with the Sisters; she dreaded the idea of returning home, and was anxiously awaiting the Archbishop's consent to be finally admitted as a novice. One day the news reached her that the longed-for consent had been refused. The good Archbishop of Lucca, Monsignor Ghilardi, did not know Gemma personally, but he had heard of her mystical experiences and of the miraculous cure. He felt that, though at present in good health, the postulant was not strong enough for the religious life. Gemma was overwhelmed with sorrow when the decision of the Archbishop was made known to her, but received it calmly, and noted it thus: "I had to leave at 5 o'clock in the afternoon of May 21, 1899. I begged the blessing of Mother Superior, and weeping said good-by to the nuns. My God, what sorrow!"[26] Father Williamson thus ends this episode of the vocation of Gemma:

"She was already habituated to sacrifice; indeed it was second nature to her, and she settled down to the quiet round of life in the home once more. On Sundays and feasts her only pleasure was to go with her little sister Giulia to the cemetery, there to pray at the tomb of her beloved parents. The hours seemed to fly while there, and the gates were often being closed before she could tear herself away from the spot. Sometimes they had to wait in the rain for the gates to open, and a good woman who lived in a cottage nearby took compassion on the two poor children and told them they would always be welcome in her house whenever they came. Gemma still hoped to be admitted to the Visitation, and often called to inquire if the Archbishop had changed his attitude, but he required four medical certificates, a thing difficult for her to obtain. The Sisters taking note also of her extreme poverty, which they found an insurmountable obstacle, began to hesitate and finally, told her that it was useless to expect to be received amongst them."

One can imagine the struggle she had to endure within her soul whenever thoughts of the future presented themselves to the mind. All she could do was to throw herself more unreservedly into the hands of Divine Providence. God was her only hope, prayer her one refuge. "Lord, what do You want of me?" she asked in her meditations, and He made her understand, gradually at first, by the usual process of frustrated hopes, and then more clearly, that He had other designs over her. Meanwhile, besides the ineffectual attempt to enter the Visitation, she tried also the Carmel, the Order of the Capuchin Sisters, and the Institute of the Mantellites, meeting invariably with refusal and disappointment. Everywhere her indifferent state of health coupled with her extreme poverty proved insuperable obstacles to the realization of the dream of her life. We guess, however, that the main difficulty lay in another direction. It had something to do with her supernatural experiences which, within the circle of nuns, were bound to excite much comment not always kind and favorable to our mystic.

In the year 1899 Pope Leo XIII ordered a mission to be given in the cities of Italy as a preparation for the opening of the new century. In fulfillment of these wishes of the Holy Father some Passionist Fathers were invited to Lucca to begin the mission in the Cathedral toward the end of June. During that month Gemma had gone daily to another church for the devotions of the Sacred Heart of Jesus. On July 10 she went to the Cathedral. At the sight of the Passionist Fathers, clothed in the habit of her dear St. Gabriel, she was deeply moved. "My impression was such," she writes, "that I cannot easily describe it. I felt inwardly attracted to them and from that time I never missed any of the sermons." On the last day of the mission she went to the closing function and received Holy Communion. During the thanksgiving our Lord said to her:

"Gemma, do you like the habit worn by the missioner?"

"It was not necessary for me to speak," she writes in the autobiography, "for my heart was throbbing and spoke for me."

"Would you like," the voice continued, "to be clothed in the same habit?"

"My God!" she exclaimed.

"You shall be the daughter of My passion, a specially beloved daughter," answered Jesus. "One of these shall be your father; go, and tell him everything."[27]

Gemma had heavenly secrets to reveal to the new confessor. The sacred wounds of the Passion of our Lord had been impressed upon her body and, notwithstanding the repeated injunctions of her angel to speak to her confessor, she had jealously kept in her heart the secret of the divine favors. The command of our Lord, however, was now too clear to be resisted. She knelt at the confessional of one of the Fathers, but, she writes: "I was unable to utter a word." The Reverend Father Gaetano of the Infant Jesus was sitting at the next confessional. Gemma knew not the Father but knelt at his feet and found she was able to narrate with great ease the whole story of her life not excluding that of her vocation to the cloister. "There are Passionist nuns," said the missioner. Gemma pondered over the words of Father Gaetano and was filled with a desire to become a Passionist. "I said this thing to my confessor," she writes, "who was well pleased and said he desired a strict rule for me. From that time my devotion to St. Gabriel increased, and I began to beg of him the grace of becoming a nun very soon." The story of Gemma's religious vocation comes to an end only with the closing days of her life. The last phase of it must be postponed in order to avoid a needless anticipation of events.

Chapter VIII

THE STIGMATA

Not by fortuitous chance had St. Francis of Assisi, sometime after the Assumption of our Lady, in the year 1224, gone to Monte Alvernia, the high mountain retreat which the Lord Orlando had many years before set apart for the use of the brethren. Something there was upon his soul which made him wistful for the uttermost seclusion. Even today, when a good road has been built to carry the pilgrim up the long ascent, and a spacious friary crowns the summit, Alvernia is awe inspiring in its remoteness from the meeting places of the world. One day, at about the Feast of the Exaltation of the Holy Cross, when his soul was more full of the love and of the sufferings of Christ, he bade brother Leo, who was allowed to visit him from time to time, to take the book of the Gospel from the altar and read the first passage upon which his eye lighted. Thrice did Leo open the book at Francis' bidding, and each time the reading concerned the Passion of our Lord.

"And then there came upon him a great longing to share in the sorrows of Christ and to have in himself that divine love which impelled Christ to suffer for men. On the following morning, he saw in vision a strange form coming toward him, whereat he was much terrified. But as this strange thing came near, and stood on a stone above him, he saw one who was a man and yet a seraph. Suddenly the seraph, who seemed in great pain and suffering, smote Francis as it were in body and soul. And then, after a moment which seemed an age, the vision disappeared."[28]

And Francis rose from his knees and stood pondering amazedly; whilst still in his soul was the mingled sorrow and joy of the vision. As he stood thus, the meaning was made clear: for in the body of Francis appeared the marks of the crucified seraph; in his hands and feet were the scars of wounds, and in the scars were the impression of nails, so formed that they might be taken for the nails of the cross. The round heads, black in appearance, protruded in the palms of the hands and on the insteps of the feet; whilst on the back of the hands and on the soles of the feet were the bended points of the nails. His right side was as though pierced by a lance. The Seraph of the vision was the spirit of the Crucified suffering through love, which now had taken entire possession of God's dear poor one; of which possession the external marks were the sign and seal.[29]

St. Francis of Assisi is the first stigmatic of whom there exists historical record. The round black heads on one side of the hands and feet, and the bended points grasping the skin on the opposite side, represented the nails in a manner that was never seen in subsequent stigmatics. The phenomenon was considered at the time so extraordinary that Brother Elias, the successor of St. Francis, thus announces it to the brethren: *"Annuntio vobis gaudium magnum et miraculi novitatem. A saeculo non est auditum tale signum praeterquam in Filio Dei, qui est Christus Deus."*[30]

After St. Francis of Assisi, about 321 stigmatics have been counted in whose stigmatization there is every reason to acknowledge the presence of Divine action. Some physiologists, even among Catholics, have maintained that the wounds might be produced in a purely natural manner by the sole action of the imagination coupled with lively emotions. When a person becomes keenly impressed by the suffering of the Savior and is penetrated by a great love, this preoccupation will act on her or him physically, reproducing the wounds of Christ. This would in no wise diminish his or her merit in accepting the trial, but the immediate cause of the phenomena would not be supernatural. Physiological science does not appear to be far enough advanced to permit a definite solution of the problem. Father Thurston, who has no reputation of being overcredulous, maintains that the arguments so far adduced in favor of natural explanations are illusory.

"They are sometimes," he says, "arbitrary hypotheses, being equivalent to mere assertions, sometimes based on exaggerated or misinterpreted facts. But if the progress of medical sciences and psychophysiology should present serious objections, it must be remembered that neither religion nor mysticism are dependent on the solution of these questions, and that in the processes of canonization stigmata do not count as incontestable miracles."

Moreover, no explanation has been offered of three circumstances presented by the stigmata of the saints: (1) Physicians do not succeed in curing these wounds. (2) On the other hand, unlike natural wounds of a certain duration, those of the stigmatics, with one exception in the case of St. Rita of Cascia, do not give forth a fetid odor nor do they fester. We have it from Signora Cecilia that once, feeling pity for Gemma's wounds, she gently bandaged them and thought no more of it. But the wounds began to cause suppuration and rankle. No sooner however were the bandages removed than the suppuration stopped, the wounds closed, leaving no scar nor any other sign on the flesh. (3) Sometimes these wounds exude perfumes, for example, those of Juana of the Cross, Franciscan prioress of Toledo, and Blessed Lucy of Narni.[31]

But though imagination cannot produce wounds like those of the stigmatics, yet it is true that it can act on the body. Even apart from the facts of consciousness, which necessarily involve some sort of interaction of body on mind and vice versa, modern psychology has thrown a flood of light on the activity of the mind on the nervous system in connection with the phenomena of fear and, in general, of emotional life. With regard to persons in abnormal condition the psychic influence on the body may produce disturbances not wholly dissimilar to those of mysticism, as is attested in many instances of hypnotic trance.

There exists, no doubt, a world of difference between the uncertain, vague, bloodlike exudations of hypnotism and the well-established, clear wounds of the mystics. The problem is nonetheless fraught with many difficulties and obscurities.

Perhaps what occurs in stigmatics is not altogether dissimilar to the phenomenon known as inspiration. An inspired book is admittedly the work of God, on whom it depends for its veracity and compelling authority. Yet the Divine Author does not make use of man as a dumb, mechanical instrument, but as a being endowed with mental and bodily powers and subject to external influences, all vitally contributing to the production of the work designed by the principal Writer. If this analogy holds good, one may assert that the imaginations and the emotions of the stigmatic may exercise a mysterious, and yet vital activity on the production of the stigmata without in any way detracting from the supernatural character of the phenomenon. Just as the legal and rabbinical genius of the Pauline letters is of St. Paul, although the letters are principally the work of God, so may we not say that the stigmata of St. Francis and of St. Gemma Galgani are partially the result of their psychic conditions, while remaining entirely supernatural in origin and character? God deals with man in all these instances, in and through his nature, and not merely on his nature. The divine action comes from outside but acts immanently; it unites itself to the human faculties and does not force them as if they were mere passive recipients of an external gift.

It may be retorted that the above explanation affords no solution of the problem, as it does not show the manner by which the mystic becomes actively responsible for the phenomena that occur in him. We admit the mysteriousness of the problem, but wish to emphasize that: (1) The above explanation shows that the difficulty extends over a wide field, covering as it does all questions of divine action in human beings, and even questions of interaction between soul and body. In other words neither physiology nor theology has so far been able to explain the contact of spirit with matter. (2) The explanation gives us assurance lest we should fear that any advance of psychophysiology and psychoanalysis may ever diminish the supernatural character of the genuine experiences of the mystics.

In relating the story of Gemma's religious vocation it became necessary to anticipate some of the events belonging to a later period of her life. We must retrace the thread of the narrative back to the time of the miraculous cure in the early spring of the year 1899. The saintly girl had passed through a series of trials and afflictions. Her heart had been purified in the crucible of sorrows and made fit to receive in greater abundance the gifts of heaven. Thus does the Divine Martyr fulfill Himself in His saints, weaning them step by step from all worldly consolations that they may find rest and happiness in the Cross of Christ. Once, during the last illness, Gemma had felt a momentary distress on account of the additional burden her malady brought upon the family. But Jesus wishing to detach her even from this natural feeling said to her: "If you were wholly dead to yourself, you would not be troubled." Since then, she yearned to live for no one else but for Jesus Crucified. It is the Cross that discriminates between the various classes of men: those to whom it is a stumbling block, those to whom it is foolishness, and those who glory in Christ's humiliations and passion. To the last-named class the Cross of Christ becomes the power and the wisdom of God to such a degree that they can make their own the cry of St. Paul: "God forbid that I should glory save in the Cross of our Lord Jesus Christ."[32]

Meanwhile the season of the Holy Week was approaching and Gemma eagerly looked forward to those days in which she could give free course to her love of the suffering Savior. During her last illness she had often been visited by Sister Giulia Sestini of St. Zita who taught Gemma the devotion of the "Holy Hour," not so popular then as it is in our own days. Gemma had made a promise to continue the practice every Thursday, if cured of her sickness. On Holy Thursday she asked and obtained permission from her confessor to begin the devotion and thus relates the experience of that blessed evening:

"I began for the first time to make the holy hour out of bed. I had promised to the Sacred Heart of Jesus that I would do so every Thursday if I recovered. I felt so full of grief on account of my sins that I experienced moments of true martyrdom. In the midst of this infinite sorrow one comfort was left to me; I could weep. It was a comfort and at the same time a relief. I passed the whole hour praying and weeping, then I sat down. My grief continued and then I felt my whole being rapt in recollection and suddenly all strength left me, so that I could scarcely get up to lock the door of my room. Where was I? I found myself before Jesus Crucified, all covered with blood. Profoundly moved by this sight I lowered my eyes. I made the sign of the Cross, and my emotion was immediately followed by a great peace; but I felt an even greater sorrow for my sins; and did not dare raise my eyes to look at Jesus. I prostrated myself on the ground and thus remained for several hours. 'Daughter,' He said to me, 'these wounds have been caused by your sins, but take comfort for they have been closed by your sorrow; sin no more. You must love Me as I have always loved you. Love Me,' He repeated several times.

"I came to myself, and from that hour the memory of the wounds of Jesus was so deeply imprinted on my mind that this remembrance has never left it since. On Good Friday morning I did not receive Holy Communion and wished to go during that day to the Church for the three hours of Agony, but I was not permitted to do so by those at home, though I was weeping. I had to make an effort, and offer this first sacrifice to Jesus. But He, always generous, wished to reward me. Locked in my room I began the three hours all alone, when there also came my Guardian Angel and together we prayed and were present at all the sufferings of Jesus. We also felt sorrow for the sufferings of our Lady. This was the first time, and the first Friday that I experienced so strongly the presence of Jesus in my soul. Though I did not receive Him in Holy Communion (as it was not possible) yet Jesus came and communicated Himself to me."[33]

On returning to herself she experienced a longing to "suffer for Jesus." Not having instruments of penance with her, she ran to the well, and, unfastening the rope she pressed it tightly around her body so as to cause her great pain. Her love for Jesus became so intense during the following days, and her desire to suffer so great that she too, like St. Catherine of Siena, St. Veronica Giuliani, and other saints, was judged worthy of bearing upon her body the wounds of Christ's Passion. One day, soon after the Archbishop's refusal to allow her to enter the convent, May 21, 1899, she turned to Jesus for consolation. "Take courage," He said, "I wait for you on Mount Calvary."

It was Thursday, June 8, 1899, the eve of the Feast of the Sacred Heart. At early dawn Gemma had gone to the church to receive Holy Communion. During the thanksgiving a sense of wonderful peace filled her soul, and Jesus spoke to her promising He would give her that very evening a signal favor. What might it be? In her simplicity she would not even try to guess. Instead she ran at once to tell the news to her confessor and to receive a general absolution from him. When evening came Gemma repaired to her room a little earlier than usual for the devotion of the holy hour.

All was silent at home and in the neighborhood. Far, beyond the hills the sun was setting in a glow of golden light. Its brightest rays, ablaze with fire and with gold, rested for a parting kiss on the pinnacles of the marble towers. All the city looked as if illuminated for a feast. Along the narrow winding streets people moved to and fro on their errands, and a few swallows, heralds of the coming summer, flitted and chirped under the eaves near a house in Via del Biscione. All the air was filled, as it were, with a sense of an impending contact with the supernatural. Gemma prayed.

"Suddenly," she writes, "I felt a piercing sorrow for my sins; but so intense that I have never experienced the like again. The sorrow was so great that I thought I must die. After that I felt all the powers of my soul sunk in recollection. My intellect knew nothing except my sins and offences against God; my memory recalled each one, and made me see all the torments Jesus had endured to save me. My will moved me to detest them and be willing to suffer anything in expiation. A world of thoughts surged through my mind; thoughts of sorrow, love, fear, hope and encouragement.

"This was quickly followed by a rapture, and I found myself in the presence of my heavenly Mother, with my Guardian Angel on her right. He commanded me to make an act of contrition, and when I had done so my Mamma said to me: 'Daughter, in the name of Jesus I forgive you all your sins,' and added, 'Jesus, my Son, loves you very much, and wishes to give you a grace. Would you know how to become worthy of it?' In my misery I knew not what to answer. Then she continued: 'I will be a mother to you; will you show yourself a true daughter?' So saying she opened her mantle and covered me with it.

"At that instant Jesus appeared with all His wounds open; blood no longer issued from those wounds but only flames of fire. Of a sudden those flames came and touched my hands, feet and heart. I felt I was dying and should have fallen had not my Mamma held me up, I being all the time covered in her mantle, and thus I remained for several hours. Afterwards, my Mamma kissed me on the forehead; then everything vanished and I found myself kneeling on the ground, but still feeling intense pain in my hands, feet and heart. I got up to go to bed and saw blood flowing from those places where I felt pain. I covered them up as best as I could and then with the help of my guardian angel, got into bed.

"The following morning I found it difficult to rise and go to church for Holy Communion. I put on a pair of gloves to hide the wounds in my hands. Owing to the intense pain I could scarcely stand and thought every moment I was dying. The pain lasted till three o'clock of Friday, feast of the Sacred Heart."[34]

This event took place on the first floor of a house numbered thirteen in the Via del Biscione, in the parish of S. Pietro Somaldi, where Gemma was living with her family. "We point to this house with singular affection," writes her future director, Father Germano, "because we believe one day it will be memorable as La Verna, where St. Francis received the stigmata."[35]

For nearly two years the stigmata continued to reappear each Thursday evening during Gemma's devotion of the Holy Hour, and remained until three o'clock on Friday afternoon. By Sunday, the wounds would have entirely healed, leaving only a slight scar. No preparation preceded this event, no sense of pain or impression of any sort, felt in those parts of the body that were to show the wounds, announced that they were imminent. There was no external sign except the recollection which preceded the ecstasy.

During the last years of her life, at the wish of Father Germano, Gemma asked and obtained from God that the marks of wounds should not appear outwardly. Their pain, however, did not cease but lasted to the day of her death.

The same Father Germano, Gemma's spiritual guide during these years and first writer of her life, gives a lengthy description of the phenomena which he often witnessed in the presence of various persons. The wounds, he tells us, were about half an inch in diameter in the palms, and on the back of the hands about five eighths of an inch long by one eighth of an inch wide. In her feet, they were not only bigger and livid around the edges, but the size of the opening was the reverse of that of the hands, that is, larger on the instep and smaller on the sole of the foot. Moreover, the wound on the instep of the right foot was as large as that on the sole of the left. Thus it would have been with our Most Holy Redeemer if both His Feet had been fastened to the Cross by one single nail. It is not safe, however, to draw any inference as to the manner of our Lord's crucifixion from the stigmata of the mystics. The phenomenon has appeared in such a variety of forms as to discountenance the arguments sometimes brought forward in favor of one's personal opinion.[36]

The wound in Gemma's side resembled in shape a half moon in a horizontal direction, with the two ends turned upward. Its length in a straight line was quite two inches, its width at the center a quarter of an inch. The stigmata have been attested upon oath by persons both learned and pious, as also by several members of the Giannini family, from whom they could hardly be entirely concealed.

Part Two

THE MYSTIC

1900-1903

Chapter IX

FROM THE OLD TO A NEW HOUSE

Who can tell what feelings crowd the heart of one who comes back, like Moses, from the intimate presence of the unseen and of celestial things? In a passing allusion St. Paul merely remarks that he "heard secret words which it is not granted to man to utter." St. Francis, singer of songs and born to carry with him the poet's sensitiveness for the sunshine and shadows of life, must needs express in verse the music of his soul.

The Praise of the Most High God

Thou art the Holy Lord and God of gods,
Alone the wond'rous in Thy works so great;
Alone art Thou the strong, the great, supreme
And Mighty Father; King of Heav'n and Earth.
The Three in One, the Fount of every good,
The Source of life and truth and love sublime.
Oh, Thine the wisdom, patience, fortitude,
The prudence and the lowliness unmatch'd,
The justice and the beauty all divine,
The gentleness extreme and sweetness fine
Are e'en O Lord, by essence ever Thine.
Our joy and gladness, peace and rest art Thou,
Our wealth and plenty, trust, security,

In storm our refuge; in temptation strength,
In danger, Thou alone, our sole defence;
On Earth our keeper Thou; through Faith and Hope,
Our bliss and life and guerdon all divine
In Heav'n through everlasting Charity.

O Goodness Infinite and endless Power
Protect me Savior sweet in my extremest hour.

Gemma was no poet. She was a lowly maid whom the Lord had drawn
to Himself. There is no record that she sang the *Magnificat* of her soul.
Instead we may well imagine her perplexity and utter confusion when,
on the morning after the stigmata, she returned home from the church
with bleeding hands and feet. How could she reveal to anyone this
wonderful thing which had come to her? Would it be wise or prudent to
speak of divine favors to persons who might not understand? But then
again, how could these signs remain altogether hidden from those with
whom she must needs live? In her simplicity she easily persuaded herself
that such marks of favor might not be too rare after all; that Jesus, perhaps, was wont to grant them to persons who loved Him. Thus encouraged she went to her Aunt Elisa, and said:

"Auntie, just look at my hands, and see what Jesus has done to me."

The good lady was amazed, almost horrified. She had felt, long before,
that there was something extraordinary, something uncanny about this
child. Her life had been quite unlike that of the other children. But the
new event seemed so strange, so utterly out of her way of looking at
things. They, the Galganis, had been honest and pious tradesmen for
generations. Miracles were surely possible in God's Church, but why
should a miracle occur in the bosom of their own family? Might it not
be a trick of Satan, of the evil eye or of a witch? She stared long at her
niece's hands, pondering not without misgivings on the destiny that lay
in store for the girl that stood bewildered before her.

Yet although the stigmata were bestowed upon Gemma while she still

abode in her parents' house, and although some of her mystical phenomena can be traced back to the time of the miraculous cure, nevertheless we feel justified in describing the period of the Saint's life, we are
now going to narrate, as in a special manner characterized by mysticism.
It was during these remaining years of her career, and in a new home,
that Gemma was raised to the highest form of contemplation: that she
experienced with ever increasing frequency the effects of supernatural
visitations in all the phases of religious feeling and emotion.

From the day when Aunt Elisa first stared on the stigmata, Gemma's life
within the family circle grew everyway more difficult. Her ecstasies and
other supernatural favors became an object of curiosity, of gossip and
mockery to the very people who could be expected to show sympathy
and consolation. Her brothers and sisters, let it be said in their excuse,
lived at this time in utter poverty. Gemma did all she could to lessen
their hardships by readiness to render the meanest services. But her calm
resignation to God's Will, her long hours of prayers, her very patience in
suffering rather exasperated their much-tried temper, and made them at
times quite unreasonable.

One of her brothers occasionally broke into blasphemies. For a soul
penetrated with the profoundest reverence for the holy Name the mere
thought of such a thing was unbearable. And yet she had to endure in
silence the sorrow of hearing blasphemies issuing from the mouths of
her dear ones. St. John Baptist Vianney, not many years before, had won
a victory against blasphemy in France. The holy curé could never allude
to this profanation of God's name without shedding copious tears, and
gave himself no rest till the last blasphemer was converted in his dear
village of Ars. Blasphemy, a remnant of early nineteenth century irreli-
gious tendencies, was, in those days, the curse of Italy too, in particular
of Tuscany so splendidly Catholic in many ways.

Once, during one of the little disputes that arise now and again in a
home, especially when tried by misfortune, her brother broke into an
unrestrained outburst of most indecent language against God and all

the saints. His profanity produced such a sense of horror in Gemma that her whole body began to sweat blood, which even trickled to the ground. She did her best to hide herself but one of her aunts, probably Aunt Elisa — "the dearest, the one that loves me most," writes Gemma to Monsignor Volpi — got so enraged on beholding the streaming blood that she rushed at her, and seizing her by the throat, exclaimed:

"It is time to end this foolery. You have given occasion enough for people to talk. If you do not tell me where this blood comes from, you shall not go out of the house again."

Gemma, who with selfless generosity always endeavored to cover up the faults of those dear to her, began to cry and replied: "It was owing to the blasphemies of my brother."

"And the blasphemies caused the blood?" "Yes, I saw Jesus suffering so much when blasphemed, that I suffered with Him and my heart poured out blood." Aunt Elisa calmed a little and said: "Is it only your brother's blasphemies that cause you this blood or those of the other people too?"

"I suffer always," answered Gemma, "but when it is he that blasphemes I suffer incredibly more."

Scenes such as this were nearly an everyday occurrence. At times she was able to lock herself in her room, or else she simply tried to distract her mind lest the people of the house should notice her agonies. "Why all this fuss for a blasphemy of your brother?" said one day Gemma's aunt on seeing her pale and about to faint. "Don't you hear blasphemies enough in this religious city of Lucca?" Gemma could only weep.

But as if all this was not enough another kind of martyrdom awaited her. Divine favors must be paid for by sacrifice and suffering. Her many ecstasies became the talk, often the object, of derision, not only at home but outside, among the backstairs idlers and gossips. "I am frightened," she writes, to her confessor, "all is known about me outside. This morning a lady friend of the house was talking of these things to my brother. They were laughing. She never left me alone this morning, from eleven to three o'clock. She worries me, and wants to know all things and brings in her school friends to whom she says mockingly: 'Come, let us go and see the ecstatic.' "

Harsh words and derision were indeed trial enough but they were at times followed by blows. One of her brothers had a taste for the theater. Being generally hard up for money, he could not always indulge in this pleasure. One evening when an exciting play was on the boards and not a coin could be found at home, the young man began to curse his destiny and dire poverty. Gemma might have kept quiet. It was the best policy under the circumstances. But how could she do so? God was grievously offended within the walls of her home. Gently and with soothing words she tried to suggest thoughts of resignation to God's Holy Will, but a big black eye was all she got for her pains.

Poor child, if only her mother had lived. Now more than ever she needed her love and support and understanding sympathy. As it was, things had become very hard to bear. Gemma prayed our Lord to take away those extraordinary manifestations, the cause of such unpleasantness. In particular she was pained because her confessor too came in for a good deal of sarcasm and quite disrespectful irony. Truly the Crucified had singled out this innocent girl as victim for the sins of others.

In reading the story of this period one cannot fail to be impressed by the strength and generosity of her character. From the month of June of that year, 1899, to the following January, she had to bear the constant vexations of people who loved but did not understand her. No privacy was possible in the midst of such surroundings and she needed it even more than the air she breathed. It was but natural to long for and seek the shelter of the convent during these months. And yet, all witnesses concur in asserting that she was ever calm, ever with a smile on her lips and love in her large, luminous eyes. No complaint, no sign of weariness or impatience has been recorded. And, as Sister Gesualda points out, it were a mistake to ascribe Gemma's superhuman endurance to natural insensibility. The intensity of feeling with which she alludes to these painful episodes in the letters to Monsignor Volpi and the language she uses in all her correspondence, reveal a temperament most sensitive to pain, most in need of human sympathy.

The reader will perhaps remember that, in obedience to the command of our Lord, Gemma had knelt at the confessional of one of the missioners in the Cathedral shortly after receiving the impression of the stigmata. He was Father Gaetano of the Infant Jesus, C.P., a man endowed with excellent gifts and a renowned preacher. Chosen to guide the first steps of our mystic he, later on, proved a source of bitter trial and many sorrows. Just now Father Gaetano is in God's hands an instrument of grace and benediction. The Passionist Fathers had no house of their own in Lucca. It was their custom, when business or the exercise of the sacred ministry called them to town, to put up in a house in Piazza di S. Maria della Rosa, where they always received the warmest reception. It was the house of the Gianninis, the house whose doors were now to open to the hard-pressed, suffering Gemma.

Cavaliere Matteo Giannini was the head of the family, an upright, thoroughly pious and goodhearted man, like to whom only few can be found in a million. The day was to come when he would have the good fortune of being present in the Vatican Basilica at the ceremony of Gemma's Beatification. As he there raised his venerable head to the altar, and saw, amid the radiance of a thousand lights, the picture of the once penniless orphan, tears of joy flowed from his eyes. They called up the memory of a well-nigh forgotten day on which he had welcomed her saying: "She will make the twelfth child God has given me." Signora Giustina, who shared in all the good qualities of her husband, gave Gemma an equally hearty welcome, and said: "We are delighted to have such an angel in our midst." So also said Don Lorenzo Agrimonti, a holy priest who lived at that time with the family.

But it is the sister of Cavaliere Matteo, the largehearted Signora Cecilia, who was to be Gemma's adopted mother, the confidante of divine secrets. To her Father Gaetano, in one of his visits to S. Maria della Rosa, spoke of the heavenly favors and of the many hardships of his penitent. How could his narrative fail to produce the desired effect? She had known the late Mr. Galgani. Like Cavaliere Matteo he was a chemist whose business had rendered an acquaintance with the Gianninis almost inevitable. Under some pretext or other Gemma was invited to dine at their house. The impression received was so good as to lead to other visits and little by little to real friendship. When the Gianninis left for Viareggio, where they used to spend the hot months of the year, Signora Cecilia, having to remain in town, requested Gemma to stay with her as a companion. From that day onward Gemma might be said to have become a member of the Giannini household. Though her people, in spite of all their troubles and difficulties, were not willing to part with her, yet from January, 1900, they allowed her to spend many days in the new home or, as Sister M. Giulia of St. Joseph tells us, in the convent of the "Mantellate." It was only in September of the same year that Gemma's relatives were finally persuaded to grant her to stay permanently with the Gianninis. Their house became indeed her shelter for the best part of the remaining three years of her life. Here, in faithful imitation of the Child Jesus in the house of Nazareth, she advanced in wisdom and age and grace before God and men.

Sanctity, now, became more than ever the conscious object of her soul's unceasing endeavors. The highest forms, too, of mystical phenomena took place during these years. These happenings were habitual as well as most extraordinary. Our Lord often appeared to her visibly after Holy Communion, so often that she could exclaim: "Jesus and I are never separated." Endowed with the gift of prophecy, she could read the hidden events of the future; she held converse with angels and saints, and went into ecstasy even while engaged in the performance of ordinary duties. Had she continued to stay with her own family, it would have been next to impossible to live in the peace and tranquility of soul she so much needed. Realizing this full well, Gemma dreaded the thought of return-

ing home even for a day. Under the circumstances, she was better sheltered here than in a convent. She was moreover fortunate in having the
wise and prudent Signora Cecilia for her intimate friend and companion
— one that knew how to guard Gemma from the intrusion of persons
whose curiosity had been stirred by the reports about the supernatural
events of her life.

Chapter X

AT HOME WITH STRANGERS

Gemma at once settled down to the new surroundings and to the daily round of household occupations. She slept but little and when, early in the morning, she heard even the least stirring of her mamma, as she affectionately used to call Signora Cecilia, rose from bed. Washing and dressing took but a few minutes, after which she was ready to start for the church. Those early hours were God's own hours during which she would not speak to anyone, for, as she said, the first fruits of the dawning day should be wholly offered to Jesus. In this matter both Gemma and Signora Cecilia, being of the same mind, rose and went to Mass long before the others woke from sleep. It was their custom to assist at two Masses, one in preparation for, the other in thanksgiving after, Holy Communion. Gemma would have stayed longer in the church and had oftentimes to be called out, but was ever ready to leave at the slightest sign from Signora Cecilia. The following words of Cavaliere Matteo, the master of the Giannini family, are worth quoting:

"Gemma was often in the company of my sister (the Signora Cecilia). On Sundays we of the family used to go out for a walk, but they remained at home spending the time in prayer and pious conversation. In the evening we all went to Benediction. Gemma never went out alone, for she used to go to church with my sister and, as far as I know, was never sent on any domestic errand. We considered her as one of the family and either my sister, or some other person, accompanied her whenever she went to her old home, to the church or to the nuns of St. Zita."

Cavaliere Matteo gives a long description of Gemma's many virtues and tells us of the love and admiration they all entertained for her.

"In winter," he says, "both she and my sister rose early and went to church at 6:30; in summer at 6. They received Holy Communion every day and they either heard two Masses or, if only one Mass was said, they remained for the corresponding time praying in the church. Gemma was never idle. At home there was a piano much used by the boys and girls. Gemma never sang nor played, although, as I came to know much later, she knew music and could sing well."[37]

On returning from the church Gemma went to help the elder girls and servants in dressing the younger children and said morning prayers with them. In childhood she had received a good education, had learned embroidery at the convent, and had attained skill in needlework; yet she always chose the humbler task of mending or knitting stockings, an occupation exceedingly useful, though generally shunned, in a house that had so large a number of children. There were other and more arduous tasks ever ready for her, such as drawing water from the well, helping the maid in cleaning and dusting, the cook in getting ready the meals and washing up dishes. If anyone fell sick, it was Gemma who undertook the entire charge of the patient as long as the illness lasted. She was the willing nurse not of the children only but also of the servant maids of the house. It is said of one of them that she made herself particularly disagreeable, never missing any opportunity of being cross and unkind to Gemma. This maid fell ill, and even then repaid the kindness of our Saint with rough manners and extremely rude behavior. Indeed she went so far as to insult her with humiliating language that reminded Gemma of her dependent position and poverty. But no amount of abuse evoked the slightest sign of resentment. In her simple way Gemma practiced to the letter the lesson of the Divine Master when He first taught mankind to love not our friends only but also our enemies.

If left to herself she would have toiled the livelong day. Her "mamma," however, loath to see her work beyond her strength, used to call her apart into the workroom, or into the open air, for a little rest or some quiet conversation. It invariably turned upon the affairs of the soul and the things of God. Ah! if we had more love for the *Volto Santo*, they would exclaim with enthusiasm, how could there still be blasphemies in Lucca?

Gemma came with the others to the common table, but did not remain long. There was no affectation in her simple way of doing penance. It all seemed so natural, so spontaneous. After taking soup, she would quietly rise and go out on the pretext of some urgent occupation. Returning later, she would partake of whatever was left on the table, help the maids in clearing away the meal, and then retire to her room leaving the others to their amusements and conversation. "Will you," she once wrote to the Director of her soul, "let me ask Jesus to take away any satisfaction in taking food as long as I live?"

From childhood her favorite virtue had been to help the poor. She found many opportunities of performing acts of charity in this devout family. The two ladies of the house often made her little presents which she accepted gladly, passing them on to the poor. And how grateful she felt to her benefactresses. She showed it, not in words alone, but by a diligent performance of the duties assigned to her. "My God," she often said, "how can I ever repay all they do for me? I do not know even how to thank them, I am so ignorant and uncultured. Make them prosper; reward them a hundredfold for their goodness. If any misfortune threatens them, let it fall on me." This generous prayer was not offered in vain. On one occasion Signora Giustina fell seriously ill and was suffering such acute pains that the doctors gave small hopes of her recovery. Gemma thought of becoming a vicarious victim, if a victim was needed. She asked God to allow her to suffer in the place of her benefactress, and her prayer was heard. Signora Giustina got well that very hour. Gemma on the other hand fell unexpectedly ill and for several months suffered the most cruel pains.

Though ever busy with some occupation or other, Gemma was nonetheless so retiring and of such a quiet disposition that it seemed as if she was never in the house. Both because of this self-imposed restraint and out of delicacy of feeling, she would at once withdraw to her private room when strangers called, so as to avoid intruding upon the conversation and hearing of matters which did not concern her. So exact was her fidelity to this rule that, at the end of the three years' stay with the Gianninis, she hardly knew a single one of the many visitors that frequently called at the house. Once Monsignor Andreucetti happened to come to the parlor whilst the family were gathered together in conversation. Gemma waited a little while, then quietly rose, and slightly bowing to the Monsignor, left the room. "Why does she run away?" asked the visitor somewhat surprised "She always does so," replied Signora Cecilia, "she never stays when people come to see us."

"Gemma belonged entirely to Jesus," is the unanimous characteristic expression of all those who came in contact with her at this period. Even the children often asked her to tell them stories of the Passion of our Lord and of the lives of the saints. The Eucharist was her principal devotion, the center of her life. "In Church," says Signora Cecilia, "she was always by my side, and knelt with her eyes fixed the whole time on the tabernacle, insensible to all other things aside from what was going on in the sanctuary. At times people, moved by her devotion, came near to ask for prayers. She did not seem to see or hear them. Having taken advice from Monsignor Volpi, I undertook to reply, assuring them that I would communicate their requests to Gemma."

Her devotion to our Blessed Lady was extraordinary. All her feasts were Gemma's feasts which she spent in prayer and holy conversations about the Blessed Virgin. Her spiritual activity, however, did not in any way interfere with the performance of domestic duties. Gemma knew how to combine work and prayer. Beyond these two occupations life had no purpose for her. As a child she had been described as proud, unsociable, and unkind by those who knew her only superficially. The same accusations she had at times to endure in the new surroundings, not indeed from those of the household, who loved her dearly, but from neighbors and visitors too worldly to understand the reasons of her reserve.

But, despite the care and affection that surrounded her, Gemma's bed was not made of roses. She was much too conscious of her dependent position and keenly felt the bitter reality of being a homeless orphan, a stranger among strangers. She courageously strove to efface herself and to hide the feelings of her heart. Even Signora Cecilia did not always realize the extent of her grief at the many misfortunes that befell her family. Only once do we discover a hint about it in a letter to her Director.

"Jesus is the owner of my heart, and belonging to Him, I find that I can smile even in the midst of tears. I am happy though encompassed by many sad happenings."

It were easy to fill pages with the numerous declarations of persons, religious and lay, who having at some time or other stayed with the Gianninis, gave sworn evidence as regards the virtues of this blessed Servant of God. It were long and wearisome to cite even a small number of them. To avoid unnecessary repetition we will be content with two statements of witnesses, in every respect of the highest authority. "With Gemma." said Signora Cecilia, "I feel a sense of quiet. Only to see her beside me makes me recollected and patient, it gives me a sense of strength, and I do not feel so much the weight of my cares. What an account I must give to God, if I do not appreciate the gift He has given me in sending this angelic girl to our house." The following testimony of Signora Giustina is even more striking. "Of Gemma, I can only say, that most wonderful things are continually happening to her, and when looking on her, I seem to behold someone not of this world. What a happiness to have had such an angel amongst us. I can affirm that the whole time she was with us, never once did the slightest trouble arise in the family on her account, nor did I ever notice any defect in her, I say no defect, not even the smallest." "That is a great thing to say," remarks Father Williamson, "when we remember that Gemma was living in the midst of eleven boys and girls, full of all the liveliness and vivacity which are typical of Italian children."

Chapter XI

MORE SUFFERINGS AND CONTRADICTIONS

The period we have just described was one also of many trials for our Saint. Reference has already been made to Father Gaetano and to the part he played in introducing Gemma to the Giannini family. On returning to Lucca, not long afterwards, he found that the conflict about the stigmata had steadily been gathering head among his friends, and that opposition to Gemma in some quarters was gaining ground day by day. He at once decided to start a thorough investigation of the case. He would leave no stone unturned; he would examine the wounds and be present at the ecstasies of the girl as often as circumstances allowed. It was important to meet Monsignor Volpi and discuss matters with him from a scientific as well as from a theological point of view. These investigations which were carried on for a long time and in the presence of many witnesses only served to shed new light upon the spiritual character of Gemma's religious experience, and to convince him all the more of its genuineness and supernatural origin. Before leaving the town he handed to Monsignor Volpi a written statement of the things witnessed during those days, and of the grounds on which he rested his opinions. It runs thus:

"I, the undersigned, hereby declare and testify that in July, 1899, I saw extraordinary wounds in the hands of the young girl Gemma Galgani. On the inside, that is, on the palms, there appeared a raised piece of flesh like the head of a nail, about as large as a half-penny; on the back of each hand there was a rather deep laceration, as if a blunt nail had been forced through the hand from the opposite side. I, and those who were with me have no hesitation in saying that the stigmata could not have been produced by natural causes. In fact on Thursday, her hands were free of any marks, on Friday they were as we have described, and again on Saturday, we found no mark except a slight reddish appearance where the wound had been."

In the light of these declarations we do not wonder if the subsequent behavior of Father Gaetano will cause surprise and admiration to the reader. It once more reveals how inconstant can be the feelings and tendencies of the human heart. From an enthusiastic admirer he first became a lukewarm believer and, step by step, one of Gemma's most uncompromising foes. His bitter opposition, which reached sometimes the level of scurrilous abuse, has never been satisfactorily explained. It was not merely the prudential skepticism of Monsignor Volpi. A more personal cause lay behind Father Gaetano's hatred. It seems that, en-lightened from above, Gemma had warned him of some secret faults of which God desired a prompt emendation. The Father did not take the admonition in good part, and from that moment started on a relent-less campaign of hostility against the innocent bearer of the heavenly message. Such complete change of attitude in a man highly placed, and esteemed for his learning and profession, had the effect of raising many doubts in the minds of Gemma's dearest friends and, we suspect, was the main reason why the doors of the Passionist Convent at Corneto were once for all closed to the saintly girl. She herself said that only on the day of Judgment would the motives of Father Gaetano's unexpected hostility be revealed. Few believed in her when she foretold his dismissal from the Order, but it proved true. His repentant return, in old age, to the religious life, was undoubtedly heaven's kind answer to Gemma's daily prayers in his behalf.

Yet the testimony left by Father Gaetano had not failed to impress Monsignor Volpi favorably toward Gemma. He knew her almost from infancy and, on many occasions, had been struck by her extraordinary virtues. Surely she could not be a conscious deceiver. Such an idea was preposterous. It had never entered his head. All the same he could not bring himself to accept the phenomena occurring under his eyes without some sort of confirmation from on high. He would hold his views in abeyance; he wanted time in order to examine the matter at leisure.

Cases of deception were not so uncommon in the history of stigmatism. He knew that through the centuries of Church history mystics and illuminati had not been wanting who had fallen from their height when, in spite of the warnings of authority, they had obstinately clung to their errors and become victims of presumption and pride. As Vicar-General of the diocese, he filled a position that lent weight and authority to his every word. He told Gemma: "I shall never believe in those fantasies and I command you to shun all these extraordinary manifestations that hinder your progress in the ordinary way of devout life." Indeed he threatened to deprive her of Holy Communion; and there was a time when very nearly he refused to hear her confession.

Meanwhile the stigmata continued to recur, every Thursday, with the regularity and precision of a physical law. Many persons of learning and piety were given opportunity to witness them. Among others there came to Lucca in August of the same year, 1899, the Provincial of the Passionists, Father Pietro-Paolo Moreschini, a holy and cultured man who became in later years Archbishop of Camerino. It was but natural that Signora Cecilia, who had begun to take interest in Gemma, should speak to him of her extraordinary religious experience. The learned Father listened in silence and expressed the desire to see the girl. The meeting was arranged to take place in the forenoon of that very day. During it the Reverend Father showed no sign of special esteem or admiration for Gemma. When, at the end, she implored him to interest himself in getting her admitted into the Passionist Convent of Corneto, he refused to have anything to do in the matter, and went so far as to use humiliating language in his remarks. Gemma gave no indication of interior distress. At the close of the interview the Father said:

"If I must concern myself with your admission into the Convent, I should first be certain of your vocation. Pray Jesus to grant me to see the two signs I myself have asked for at this very moment."

These were the sweat of blood and the stigmata. At about half past two in the afternoon of that day. Gemma, according to custom, went to pray before a large crucifix that stood against the wall of the Giannini's dining room.

Often she had fallen into ecstasy while looking at that image of the Savior and often, too, she had been miraculously raised from the ground and been allowed to kiss the Sacred Wounds of Him who died for mankind. Once in September, 1901, while busy with some housework her eyes turned, now and again, to the great crucifix, as if drawn thereto by an inner irresistible force. It called her. "Jesus," she said, at last, unable to bear any longer the flame of love burning within her soul, "let me come to You, I die of Your love." Suddenly the figure of Christ began to stir with life and stretched forth one arm inviting her to go to Him. Borne on the wings of love she rose to His embrace. For a little while there she stood, as one resting on clouds, to drink with her lips from the fountain of love divine. In memory of this event the light of a ruby lamp now glows, day and night, before that image of the crucifix on the wall of the dining room of Casa Giannini. It is held in great veneration by the faithful.[38]

Signora Cecilia, who in the present instance had divined the motive of Gemma's going apart to pray, noiselessly came to the door and saw her in ecstasy. She made a sign for the Father to follow her. The face of the ecstatic was pale and motionless, like that of a corpse. A sweat of blood flowed from her eyes, nose, mouth, and ears as well as from the hands. It continued to flow for full half an hour. In the course of the afternoon Gemma, who had returned to her senses, said to Signora Cecilia: "The Father has asked for two signs of Jesus. One He has already given and He will also give the other. What could the second sign be?" The Signora did not reply but on meeting the Provincial at about five o'clock she said:

"Father, perhaps the other sign you prayed for is the stigmata?"

"Why do you ask me?" he exclaimed with great surprise.

"Because," she answered, "I have seen two red marks appear in the hands of Gemma. They are like those she has every Thursday."

At supper Gemma ate less than usual and soon found an opportunity to withdraw to her room. The ever watchful Signora Cecilia at once read in Gemma's illuminated face the clear indication of an impending miracle. After supper she invited the Father and Don Agrimonti to enter the room. This is what the Passionist Provincial stated in the Process for Gemma's Beatification:

"The head of the girl was flexible but without movement. Her face was corpselike, the hands seemed contracted and I saw in the middle of each palm as well as on the corresponding back of the hand, a wound of oval shape and about a centimeter in size. Round the head I saw drops of blood especially over the brows. The phenomenon lasted ten minutes after which the skin resumed its natural color except for a few drops of blood staining the hands."

In a letter from Florence to Monsignor Volpi, a few days later, the same Father wrote:

"I saw with my own eyes the wounds in her hands, both in the palms and on the back of the hands. They were really rent open. After the ecstasy they healed up and only a slight scar remained. How could such wounds thus heal immediately by mere natural means? I do not hesitate to say that it is the work of God, and the more so, because this girl is extremely humble, obedient, innocent and has a great love of suffering. I am still of opinion that you should provisionally place her in a convent, for the many reasons of which you are aware."

Notwithstanding this judgment of Father Provincial, Monsignor Volpi was still loath to recognize God's finger in these events without even clearer proof. He would not be lightly budged from the path of prudence. In particular he desired that these manifestations, whether divine or diabolical, should cease and ordered Gemma to keep clear of them. The latter strove her best to obey. Like St. Aloysius, who was ordered to follow in his devotions the accepted maxim of asceticism *Deum propter Deum esse relinquendum*, that we must leave God for the sake of God, she would seek distraction in prayer and timidly drive away the thought of God, afraid to fall into ecstasy. The effort was not always successful.

"These things." she wrote, "seem as impossible to me as they do to you but, please, do not blame me for this. I do not want them ... I say to Jesus: 'See, my Jesus, if You had dealt less generously with me, and had loved me less. I might not have loved You so much ... As it is I cannot exist without You: if it be truly You, make it known to everybody. But if it is the work of the evil one, I wish to have nothing to do with it.' "

Again and again she has recourse to Him to still the storm that raged in her agitated soul. He reproached her for doubting. Gemma replied: "I doubt, because others doubt," but "Jesus, if it be You, make them understand. In the present circumstances we are helpless — I, the confessor and all those, who have knowledge of these things."

Monsignor Volpi who seems to have personified in himself the spirit of his age made up his mind to clear his doubts by a definite recourse to men of science. He told Signora Cecilia, who faithfully used to report to him the events of each week, that he would call on a Friday to have the stigmata examined by a doctor. The arrangement was kept secret from all. But He who penetrates into the inmost recesses of our thoughts, revealed the secret to Gemma and commanded her to signify to the confessor that, whatever sign he asked would be given, provided he came alone. In the presence of the doctor nothing would happen. It fell out as Gemma had foreseen.

On September 8, Feast of Our Lady's Nativity, which that year occurred on a Friday, she went into an ecstasy shortly after one o'clock. Blood was flowing from her head as well as from the open wounds on the hands. Cavaliere Giannini together with his wife and Signora Cecilia were there looking with bated breath and eyes full of wonder. Quite unexpectedly, at about two o'clock, Monsignor Volpi and a doctor entered the room. The latter, after a few minutes' observation, dipped a towel in water and washed the head and the hands of the ecstatic. Straightway the blood stopped and no trace of wounds could any longer be seen.

"There," exclaimed the doctor, "it is all the effect of hysteria. When suffering from this disease, they do these things. They make the blood flow by means of pins and needles."

"No," rejoined Monsignor Volpi with vehemence, "I cannot think this child capable of such mean tricks."

Poor Gemma! Far away from the things of earth and intent on the drama of Calvary that was being enacted before her mind's eye, she was wholly unconscious of the events taking place around her. The doctor's sneer, the confessor's doubts, the anguish and pain of Signora Cecilia and Cavaliere Giannini were for the moment withheld. With unseeing eyes she still looked upon them all wrapped up in a prayer of oblation, offering herself to be nailed to the cross with Jesus. It was surely in answer to this petition that, toward the end of the ecstasy, she saw in a vision the coldness, the doubts, and the scarcely conceived disappointment lurking in the heart of those around her. How shall we describe the feelings of disillusion that passed in her soul when she first consciously stood before the circle of the bewildered friends? Referring to it in a letter to Father Germano, she writes:

"One thought I was a somnambulist; others that I was suffering from some illness; others that I myself had made the wounds in my hands and feet."

Our Lord assured her that these trials had been permitted by Him and would be followed by trials even more painful, but He added: "I shall give you a new spiritual Director by whose aid Monsignor Volpi will be won over to your side."

Toward evening Signora Cecilia went out of the house for a stroll and for a breath of fresh air. She took Gemma as a companion. They had not gone far when the latter timidly said: "Will you, please, take me to Jesus in the Blessed Sacrament. I need Him." They entered a church nearby and prayed for nearly an hour during which Signora Cecilia never withdrew her eyes from her ecstatic companion. "I would say something to you but I am so ashamed of myself," Gemma said on coming out of the church, and added: "Look at my hands." They were bleeding and there appeared on them two clear wounds. Monsignor Volpi, to whom Gemma was taken, saw the blood and attentively examined the wounds but expressed no opinion. Outwardly he was still incredulous, but in his heart he could no longer deny that appearances were all against him. Later he wrote:

"I must confess I felt as if in the presence of a supernatural fact, the more so that, as I was assured, the following day the wounds had disappeared. Today, after some years of experience I am convinced that God permits at times these extraordinary phenomena to give to men a manifest proof of His interior workings in the souls of those whom He loves in a special manner."

To St. Francis, the stigmata were not a mere personal gift. They had in his case a public, almost an official significance. They stood as a voice from heaven, a witness to the mission that had been entrusted to him for the spiritual uplift of a morally depraved society. His, however, was an age of faith which saw no reasons to disbelieve in the existence of the supernatural simply because this world is so entrancingly beautiful, and is governed by wise and wonderful laws. But Gemma Galgani belonged to a more incredulous epoch. The nineteenth century, in the flush of its new and most marvelous discoveries, rejected the old faith. Men of science, assuming the absolute self-sufficiency of the physical laws (often man-made systems of categories contrived in a vain attempt to pierce the mystery of reality), refused to admit facts that lay outside the sphere of space and time, and so seemed to them foreign to the grasp of the limited perception of our senses. Even today many such men will not accept the wonders of Theresa Neumann of Konnersreuth, not because of a conviction arrived at after a careful investigation of the phenomena, but, a priori, because of their miraculous character. Verily one needs the reverential spirit to receive a prophet's words as well as to test the evidence of a miracle. Both are divine messages that make no appeal to a prejudiced mind. The burning bush of Mount Horeb can only be approached by pulling off the shoes from one's feet.

> Science advances with gigantic strides.
> But are we aught enriched in love and meekness.

Gemma's preternatural experiences were more similar in purpose, and in immediate result, to those of Theresa Neumann than to those of St. Francis. At first sight they seemed to fulfill no other function than that of being an object of scorn and a sign of contradiction. Maybe their only purpose was to show to the world that even a life of simplicity and obscurity can go hand in hand with the possession of gifts usually reserved to seers and great leaders in the Church. Be that as it may, God wished to hide Gemma Galgani's secrets in His own Divine Heart, while she, on her part, being naturally averse to the limelight of publicity, shrank from any display of these privileges before others, and in a special manner before strangers.

"If the manuscripts must fall into the hands of that specialist, O Lord, make him see only blank paper!" she exclaimed, and blank paper was all that the specialist saw when her writings were brought to him for examination.[39]

Chapter XII

THE MEETING WITH FATHER GERMANO

Left a widow at twenty-eight, Jane Frances de Chantal took a vow of chastity and besought the Almighty in all her prayers to send her a spiritual guide. One morning, when the air was fresh and sweet, for the spring was toward, and she was riding in the forest of Bourbilly, the scene of her widowhood tragedy, she ardently conceived a desire of giving herself entirely to God. Suddenly before her she beheld in a vision the majestic figure of a gentle and kindly prelate. At the same time an interior voice pointed him out to her as the heavenly guide held in reserve for the direction of her soul. Three years later, during the Lent of 1604, the Baroness visited her father at Dijou, where St. Francis de Sales was preaching at the Sainte Chapelle. In him she recognized the mysterious personage of Bourbilly and placed herself under his guidance. Then began that much-admired correspondence between the two Saints which determined the vocation of Jane Frances de Chantal, and led up to the establishing of the religious order of the Visitation.

Strange to say an almost identical favor was vouchsafed to the lowly maiden of Lucca. In the hours of her distress, forsaken by those who had the spiritual charge of her soul, she turned for comfort and light to Jesus in the Blessed Sacrament. Her prayer was instantly heard. The Divine Savior appeared in a vision, not alone, but in the company of an aged, venerable priest, whom He introduced to her by name as the future director chosen for her guidance. At the sight of him, she was filled with joy.[40] But Gemma had an instinctive fear of illusions through which even holy persons may fall a prey to morbid devotions and the deceits of the evil spirit. She, therefore, at the first opportunity, spoke to Monsignor Volpi of the aged priest seen in the vision and of the promise made to her by our Lord. Would he give permission to write to the newly appointed director? The prelate ever cautious and temporizing thought it more prudent to wait a little while before consenting to her request. Two letters of the Blessed tell us the story of what followed.

On January 29, 1900, she wrote to Father Germano, who was the guide to whom our Lord had referred.[41]

"For a long time I have desired to see you, and also to write to you. I asked my confessor for leave to write but he always said 'no.' Last Saturday I asked again and he said 'yes,' which gave me great consolation. But as I begin to write a great fear comes over me: this is because I have such strange things to tell that even you will be surprised. I shall say it frankly that my head is a bit strange, for, sometimes, I fancy I see or hear impossible things. I say impossible because Jesus has never before appeared to souls as sinful as mine."

In this letter, which is very long and covers twelve pages of letter paper, she gives a minute account of all that had happened during the last two years; of her serious illness and miraculous cure by St. Gabriel, her religious vocation and her first meeting with the Passionists; of a Convent of Passionist nuns which would later on be founded in Lucca, of which she gives many details as if it were actually before her eyes.

A little later she wrote a second letter to the same Father in which she says:

"Yesterday I was before Jesus in the Tabernacle. I was called, I think, by Jesus. (Father, before reading further I beg you not to believe anything. I only write from obedience, otherwise I should not say a word.) He said: 'Write, and tell the Father that your confessor will be glad to be put in communication with him. He will do it, for it is My will.' "

These revelations and commands of our Lord led, in the end, to a long correspondence between Father Germano and Monsignor Volpi, who was glad to share his responsibility in the direction of Gemma with one so well versed in mystical theology and with so high a reputation for piety.

Father Germano at the request of Monsignor Volpi, came to Lucca sometime in September of 1900. His arrival was not known to Gemma who, nevertheless, recognized him at once and greeted him with joy. On seeing her, he too felt in his soul a lively sense of devotion for her, as if in the presence of some heavenly being. They both entered the chapel and prayed for a long time.

Gemma's first biographer gives here a detailed description of an episode that shows the Saint in an entirely new light. In her younger days, as we have stated elsewhere, people had thought her narrow, self-centered, intent only in the practice of what Father Faber has beautifully called "the little virtues" (they form in reality the kernel of a devout life, the very warp and woof of holiness). In this episode her figure rises to the mountaintops of Christian zeal where live the missionaries and great apostles of charity. Like her spiritual sister, Thérèse of Lisieux, she too, in the solitude of the house in Piazza di S. Maria della Rosa, can emulate the spirit of St. Francis Xavier. As a child she had foretold the conversion of a sinner for whom, along with the playmates of the school, she had prayed during the rehearsal of a drama. She is now seen in the limelight of a martyr ready to shed her blood and to suffer all the torments human flesh can endure, if by them, men can be brought nearer to God. In this striking episode Gemma wrestles as did Jacob when he fought with the Angel and said: "I will not let thee go except thou bless me."[42] She is fighting for the eternal salvation of a sinner. But let us leave the narrative to Father Germano.[43]

"It was on a Thursday. About the middle of supper, Gemma, feeling she was about to fall into ecstasy, got up from the table and went to her room. A little after Signora Cecilia came and called me. I went and found Gemma in ecstasy. The subject of this ecstasy was the conversion of a sinner, and took the form of a contest, between the young girl and the Divine Justice, to obtain his conversion. Never have I been present at so moving a spectacle. The dear child was sitting on her bed with her whole person turned toward a corner in the room where she saw our Lord. She was not agitated, but earnest and resolute like one engaged in a conflict and determined to win at any cost.

" 'As You have come, Jesus,' she said, 'I renew my supplication for my sinner. He is Your son and my brother. Save him. Jesus!' (Here she mentioned his name.) He was a stranger whom she had come to know in Lucca and, moved by an interior inspiration had many times, by word and by writing, urged him to follow the dictates of his conscience and not to content himself with being considered a good Christian.

"But Jesus showed Himself disposed to act as the strict Judge and remained unmoved by her pleading. 'Why do You not heed me today, Jesus? For one soul alone You have done so much, so why will You not save him? Save him, Jesus, save him. Be pitiful, Jesus. Do not answer me so. In Your mouth, as You are mercy itself, the word abandon sounds strangely. You did not count the number of their sins.'

"The Lord showed her why He did not yield. He manifested to her, one by one, the sins with all the circumstances of time and place, which this sinner had committed, and showed her that they were beyond measure. For a moment the young girl appeared overwhelmed, her arms fell and she gave forth a deep sigh, as if she had given up all hope. But recovering she renewed the attack: 'I know it, I know it. I know he has sinned much, but I have sinned more. Yes. I admit I am not worthy to be heard, but I present another mediatrix on behalf of my sinner. It is Your Mother herself who prays for him. Oh, will You say no to Your Mother? Surely You cannot say no to her. And now, answer me, Jesus, and say You have saved my sinner.'

"The scene changed, the Savior granted the grace and with indescribable joy Gemma exclaimed: 'He is saved. He is saved; Jesus, You have conquered; triumph always thus.' And then she came out of the ecstasy. This moving scene lasted about half an hour, and after it was over, I returned to my room where my mind was filled with a thousand thoughts. Suddenly I heard a knock at my door. 'A stranger wishes to see you, Father.' He was shown in and fell on his knees at my feet weeping, and said to me: 'Father, I want to make my confession.' It was Gemma's sinner converted at that very moment. He accused himself of all the sins which I knew from hearing Gemma repeat them in her ecstasy. One only he forgot, of which I was able to remind him. I consoled him, and told him what had happened a little before, asking him to let me make known this wonderful grace. After a mutual embrace we both parted."

Appointed, as we have seen, by miraculous intervention to be spiritual director of Gemma, Father Germano seriously began the study of her character and pursued it with unremitting zeal for about three years. He put his pupil to many lengthy tests and left no stone unturned in order to reach a right decision regarding her. Monsignor Volpi was fully satisfied and happy that such an experienced man in things appertaining to the soul had undertaken her spiritual direction. Gemma, who more than anybody else was glad of the new arrangement, waited calmly the decision of her new director. This was not long in coming. It took off a great load from her soul, for Father Germano wrote assuring her that what had happened was really from God and that she could safely allow herself to be led by the Holy Spirit in that way. Her gratitude knew no bounds. In one of her letters she wrote:

"O Father, what infinite thanks I owe you for all the care you take of my poor soul. If I succeed in saving it you will see what I shall do for you. When I have reached heaven I shall draw you after me at any cost ... If you only knew how much good your letters do me! I hope by this time you know me well."

Commenting on this passage Father Germano remarks that Gemma's direction was carried on chiefly by means of letters, and he continues:

"But by God's disposition of things I had the opportunity of going on many occasions to Lucca, and while, staying at the Gianninis, had every facility of helping her and continuing my examination of her spirit. She was humble, docile, lovable, ready for any sacrifice, and full of the love of God, yet at the same time so natural that you would scarcely distinguish her from any ordinary girl of her own age.

"She had a remarkable simplicity which ran through all her actions; this simplicity was manifested in her dress, her carriage and her speech. In church, where she spent hours before the Tabernacle, there was nothing singular in her attitude, not a sigh, not a movement out of the common. For Gemma faith almost appeared to be sight. She spoke to God with a confidence and abandon such as a little girl would show toward her father."

Yet even now a certain amount of doubt and hesitation still remained with Monsignor Volpi. The idea of getting scientific aid to solve his doubts lingered in his mind. This we can notice from the letters of Father Germano. The latter thus wrote to him:

"There is no trace of hysteria in Gemma. If you would judge exactly of the external facts concerning her, do not take them separately, but take them together, and you will find a marvelous agreement between them. Hysteria, on the contrary, has for its substantial form, volubility, inconstancy, lightness, futility, restlessness, etc., because hysteria is synonymous with insanity, and one whose head is so affected, is never consistent with himself."

In another letter addressed to Monsignor Volpi on March 4, 1901, Father Germano writes:

"God has entrusted this soul to you and not to others. Do not think of doctors. I warn you before God that the consequences would be very harmful; and as to the spirit of Gemma, you see what miracles God has performed to keep her hidden. In the midst of a numerous family she passes unobserved, and shall we make everything public? A priest will speak (of course in confidence) to another priest, the doctor to his wife, and thus it will be carried from mouth to mouth, through the *piazzas* and *cafés*, and then it will become a show like that of *Bois d'Haine*, of L. Lateau and Orisa, and finally end in the Holy Office. Do not trust anyone. The wonderful things which happen to Gemma take place amidst great tranquility. But you may say there are doubts. Do you doubt still? Then, go and see with your own eyes. The best rule by which to judge Gemma is her interior state. The external facts I leave out of account. That which impresses everyone is the simplicity, profound humility, detachment, union with God, the abandon, level headedness, desire of suffering, and the unaffected behavior of this little girl in the midst of so many extraordinary things."

Writing also to Signora Cecilia, on July 1, 1901, Father Germano said:

"As regards this dear little girl, do not be the least disturbed. It is certain that it is all the work of God, and that God will bring it to completion in spite of the ignorance and passions of men and all the rage of the devil ... I congratulate you on being chosen by God to protect and look after her. You will be abundantly rewarded."

Chapter XIII

GEMMA'S HEROIC VIRTUES

The writer of these pages has been anxious to break as little as possible the continuity of historical facts. The last three years of Gemma's life are years of no special historical interest, though crowded with ecstasies and apparitions from celestial beings. She is lifted to regions where the air is purer and the heavens nearer; she is filled with light from above and adorned with marvelous gifts. During the same period, for such is the story of the saints, she has to endure a veritable martyrdom of pain. Temptations of the most alluring kind assail her and every divine apparition is counterbalanced by vexations from, and strange manifestations of, the evil spirit. Under the circumstances we shall no longer follow Gemma's life year by year, a method which would lead to mere repetition of the same phenomena recurring over and over again during the remaining period of time. Perhaps, too, our narrative may gain in novelty and interest if for the chronological arrangement we substitute here the description of spiritual occurrences, setting them forth in different chapters as we proceed with the story of Gemma's life. One thing the reader is asked to do. He must bear well in mind that the spiritual events which he shall find grouped together into a single chapter, or the part of a chapter, must be spaced out by his imagination as having taken place, not all at once, but during a period of three years.

Before, however, describing these events it is important that we dwell at some length on the virtues of our Saint. This becomes all the more necessary because extraordinary gifts, or what theologians call *gratiae gratis datae*, favors freely bestowed, are of themselves insufficient to establish a title to sanctity and canonization. Historically they are known to have been found sometimes in unworthy persons, nor can they always be distinguished from the mental illusions of abnormal sensibility and neurosis. In the decree concerning the virtues of our Saint no mention is made of these extraordinary gifts. They have not been singly approved by the Church although the canonization itself must be assumed as a recognition, in a general way, of their supernatural character.

"As far as I know," wrote one of the witnesses, "Gemma Galgani practiced all virtues in a heroic degree."

Once, as she lay on her sickbed, a nursing Sister asked her which virtue was most important and most dear to God. Without a moment's hesitation, she answered: "Humility, humility: for it is the foundation of all the rest." Though young she realized what many pious persons fail to grasp even in mature age, that God reserves to Himself praise for the gifts with which He favors us. It is His will to have the sole glory of them. Not for vain display does He confer blessings upon us, but to manifest His goodness. One of the permanent miracles in the life of Gemma was her total distrust of her own sufficiency, and the profound conviction that from God alone could she derive the strength, no less than the light, she needed.

"From the moment I was called to examine her spirit," writes Father Germano, "I made humility the test by which to judge her and I found her sanctity fully proved when judged by this standard." Her letters always concluded with the same formula, "Your poor Gemma." With that formula she signed them all as with a saving talisman. Father Germano had asked her to sign the letters she wrote to him not "Your poor Gemma" but "Gemma of Jesus." She tried to obey but failed in her endeavor, and once more reverted to the formula of old. Even in her ecstasies, when wholly rapt out of her senses, she spoke of herself as a wretched sinner and a despicable worm.

Not only had Gemma a low opinion of herself, she also wished that others should share this opinion, and she, therefore, studiously endeavored to hide whatever might redound to her credit. She has been described as possessing a clear and alert intellect, great strength of mind, and a resolute will. Yet dealing with her you might have been led to think she had no will of her own; for she sought the advice and the direction of others in almost everything. At school she had carried off prizes in French, drawing, and painting; but after leaving school, she never made a display of her French, nor was ever seen to take brush or pencil in hand. Endowed with a large fund of common sense, Gemma would not have been overscrupulous in making use of these attainments but for the change in her family circumstances. Once the rich daughter of a prosperous citizen of Lucca, she had now fallen on evil days, and it seemed more appropriate in the present circumstances to abstain from a show of talents which had become her well in the days of ease and plenty.

One day, while her director was in the house, a prelate came to see her. Having reason to suspect that this dignitary of the Church entertained some high opinion of her, Gemma would willingly have remained in her chamber. As things stood, she had no alternative but to present herself before him. Her humility, however, prompted her to have recourse to an artifice, which, she hoped, would disabuse his mind of any too favorable notion that he might have entertained of her sanctity. She took into her arms a big cat which was in the house, a thing she had never been known to do before, and so, tenderly caressing it, she appeared before him. The trick was a perfect success. The good prelate shrugged his shoulders in contempt: while Gemma, still hugging her cat, tripped quietly away, without making the least obeisance to her visitor.

"If I at times," she once wrote to Father Germano, "experience happy moments, it is when people despise me and consider me a fool."

"Pride," she remarked on one occasion, "is the sin of the devil; to be Jesus' friend we should be humble, very humble."

Much the same may be said of the virtue of obedience, which this saintly girl practiced with childlike simplicity throughout her life. On entering the house of Cavaliere Matteo she made it a point to carry out every injunction of her new superiors, even in matters of no great importance. Signora Cecilia had only to say: "Gemma, get up, let us go out"; or "Go back, to your room." and without a word she would instantly do what was commanded.

In her ecstasies, though insensible to everything else, Gemma's obedience was remarkable. Signora Cecilia writes: "Once after Holy Communion I called Gemma to come back to her place, but she was already in ecstasy. Fearing others might notice it, I said within myself: 'O Jesus, if it be Your will, make her return to her place by obedience.' Would you believe it? She raised her head at once. I signed her to go to her place, which she did. Finding this plan so successful, I afterwards continued it many a time, and God always made her obey."

Father Germano, however, had a still stranger experience of the miraculous in Gemma's obedience. Once, when she was ill, he happened to be in her room with other persons, and wishing to put her obedience to the test, he said to her: "Here, take my blessing: fall asleep, and we will retire." He had scarcely finished speaking when she turned round in the bed and was soon in a profound slumber. He then fell on his knees, and, lifting his eyes to heaven, gave her a purely mental command to awake. She at once awoke and turned toward him with her usual sweet smile, but the good Father reproved her.

"Is this how you obey; did I not tell you to sleep?"

"Father," she answered humbly, "you must not be angry; I felt a tap on my shoulder, while a voice cried aloud: 'Up, the Father calls you.' "

It was her Guardian Angel, adds Father Germano, who was watching by her bedside.[44]

Obedience is not generally considered by novices in the spiritual life as a very difficult virtue. In religion, the younger members of the house regard it as the easiest of the three vows. May God spare them those not uncommon situations of later years when obedience must needs become the touchstone of religious heroism. It is significant that St. Paul singles out the obedience of Jesus Christ for special mention and emphasis: "He humbled Himself becoming obedient unto death, even unto the death of the cross."[45] Gemma's perfect obedience did not arise from timidity, dullness, or indecision of character. By temperament and early education she was more inclined to command than to obey, and the ease with which she submitted to others was the fruit of a rigorous self-suppression. Her hardest struggle in the pursuit of this virtue lay in the resistance she had to offer to the frequent apparitions of our Lord in accordance with the direction of her confessor. Oftentimes, the ecstasy overtook her before she became aware of it. This is how she describes graphically one of her victories in a letter to the spiritual director: "I rose quickly and fled; I left Jesus, obeyed and was at peace."

Asceticism is at a discount in the modern world. For the old hero-ic motto *abstine et sustine*, abstain and sustain, new slogans have been substituted, better suited to a generation that has lost its hold on spiritual ideals and sunk into the materialism of a neopagan world. Pleasure has become nowadays the supreme end of life; the one god deserving service and adoration. All this is far from being new. Hedonism has always found numerous adepts among men. What is new in history is the boastful pride that some moderns take in their hedonism. In the past, pleasure seekers knew at least they were following the downward lead of their senses rather than the upward guidance of their reason. They knew they were sinners. In our days ideas have changed. It is the "good timers" who pretend to be wise, and pious Christians are almost expected to apologize for their old-fashioned principles and conduct.

Even among Catholics the old asceticism is looked upon with disfavor. There is an erroneous theory, that for some time went under the specious name of Americanism, by which it is held that Christian asceticism should be associated exclusively with active virtues, such as generosity, medical beneficence, teaching or social cooperation, and that men should eliminate inexorably, as useless, the so-called passive virtues consisting in mortifications, penances, fasts. A grave error this, in perfect antithesis to the traditional teaching of the Church and the psychological individual experience. Our Lord Jesus Christ has preached and severely practiced the mortification of the flesh and of the senses. St. Paul feels the obligation of chastising his body for fear that he may be lost. The saints of every age, clime, and country down to our own time, have passionately loved the mortification of the senses.

With Gemma Galgani the chastening of the flesh began from the very dawn of adolescence. Even at that early period she began an incessant war against her innocent body, and against her senses over which she vowed to keep the most rigorous and constant watch. Like Aloysius Gonzaga she scrupulously avoided looking straight into the face of persons she might be speaking to. All pleasures, however small and innocent, were banned from the scheme of life she had early chalked out for herself. Reference has already been made to the permission asked of her spiritual director that she might "ask Jesus to take away any satisfaction in taking food as long as I live." She used many industries to reduce as much as possible, without attracting notice, the quantity of food necessary to keep body and soul together. One little device she had found which may raise a smile, but let us be cautious lest in our puny conceits we seek to dictate to the saints the ways of pleasing and serving the Lord. She kept a spoon exclusively for her own use. It had a hole in the middle that served the double purpose of letting her appear to be long enough at the soup and allowing her free scope for mortification.[46] Speaking of the mysterious illness of which Gemma was in the end miraculously cured the specialist Dr. Tommasi stated:

"I made the operation. The sick girl never spoke; she was free to move her head and other limbs but never allowed herself the least motion that would give her relief from pain. It was like operating on a dead body. Yet she must have suffered much. When the operation was over I asked her: 'Have you suffered much?' She replied with a smile as if to say: 'A little.' And I remember well I gave no anesthetic."[47]

Occasions to practice mortification arose almost every day in the latter part of Gemma's life when, on account of the extraordinary events that surrounded her, she was liable to be treated by unfeeling neighbors as a hysterical person, or as one possessed by the devil. The assistants at St. Michael's parish church, in particular, were wont to be rude to her. They would make her wait when she asked to speak to her confessor. At times they would mock and call her a hysteric. Once their bad manners carried them much too far. Gemma had come to the church with a girlfriend desirous to see Monsignor Volpi who had just entered with other canons of the Basilica. "Send her away," said loudly a voice from the clerical circle, "send her away to tell her stories to some other priest." The poor girl felt the keenness of the remark, but tried to put up patiently with it and withdrew. Writing to her spiritual director she incidentally mentions the episode and says: "I felt ashamed, but thought of Jesus and made nothing of the affair."

On another occasion a young man met her as she was going to church with the Gianninis. Moved I do not know by what evil spirit the stranger came near, insulted her, and spat in her face. Gemma remained quiet and wiping her face with a handkerchief said: "Well, I wish to become a saint in spite of the world and of satan."

The Old Testament has given saints, but not virgins, to heaven. This rarest of virtues is a jewel which Christ brought to earth to mark the beginning of a new covenant with mankind, the covenant of the spirit and of love. Strange, whilst the maidens of Israel sought in their marriage dream hopes of a messianic motherhood, Christ's first gift to the regenerated world was to enter it by the instrumentality of a Virgin Mother.

Purity was indeed Gemma's most precious jewel. When speaking of their orphan ward among themselves, the members of the Giannini family, especially Signora Cecilia and Signora Giustina, used to refer to her as "the dear angel." Even as a child she avoided being touched by others and shrank from the most innocent caresses and affectionate kisses of her father. She looked with instinctive horror upon all occasions of temptation, regarding them as dangers to the purity of her soul and insidious snares, which the evil spirit laid along her path toward the attainment of perfect purity. In later years she would never use a looking glass, even when doing up her hair, or wiping away the bloodstains which flowed from the crown of thorns on her head. "I would rather be blind," she once said, "I would rather be deprived of all my senses than that they should in the slightest degree become the occasion of sin." "What is the use of a looking glass," she would playfully say, "what is the use of a looking glass to an orphan who wishes to belong entirely to Jesus?" Early in life she had started the practice of saying every day three "Hail Marys" with the hands under her knees. One day Aunt Elisa, who was perhaps spying on Gemma a little more than necessary, finding her in that particular posture, asked: "Now, Gemma, why are you praying that way?" "It was grandmamma who taught me when I was quite a child," replied Gemma, and added: "She said that if we pray to our blessed Lady so, she would never allow us to commit the slightest sin against holy purity." Many witnesses testify to having felt a heavenly perfume on entering the Gianninis' house all the time Gemma lived there, and all attribute this supernatural fragrance to her angelic purity.

In a similar strain we might dwell on this holy girl's love for poverty, spirit of penance and charity. The simplicity of her dress had become proverbial. Lucca shall ever remember Gemma's *mantellette* under which, when going out of the house, she invariably kept her hands, often enough to hide the stigmata. Her hat, to which she ever contrived to give an out-of-fashion touch, had become an object of comment to the smart maidens of the town. Cavaliere Matteo confessed he was, at times, ashamed to go out of the house when Gemma made one of the company because, as he put it, "she was so ridiculously dressed." And yet Gemma was noted for the simplicity of her dress and deportment. She was not really ridiculous in her way of dressing, but did not want to wear the fashionable clothes of the girls of her age. Whenever such clothes were presented to her, she found a way of exchanging them for older ones, or passed them on to the poor.

"In her pockets," Signora Cecilia once remarked, "I never find anything except the rosary beads and the pocket handkerchief." When presents of money, food, or clothes were made to her by friends or relatives she would receive them with a grateful smile because, as she playfully remarked, "she could thus afford to be munificent to the poor." Indeed she used to stint herself of food in order to have more of it to give away. The first day of every month was Gemma's day of special joy since her aunt of Camaiore used to send ten lire, which before sunset found their way into the pockets of the sick and the needy. A girl, San-drina Maggi, tells this beautiful anecdote:

"One evening I was walking with Gemma along the Via del Vado when we met an old lady who was shivering with cold for want of proper clothes. Gemma had just received from one of her aunts a heavy woolen undergarment. Quietly she withdrew behind a door, removed the under-garment and gave it to the old lady saying: "Pray for me that Jesus may warm me with the fire of His love.' "

Gemma's penance was continuous. She wore twisted ropes with knots around her waist and, with many devices of her own invention, managed to render uncomfortable even the few hours of sleep she allowed to her-self. Monsignor Volpi, and later Father Germano, had to take away from her those instruments of penance with which she contrived to chastise her innocent body and render it, in the words of St. Paul, obedient to the soul.

The following testimony of Sister Gemma of the Visitation, whom we shall presently know in this book as Euphemia Giannini, an intimate friend and the confidante of our Saint, shall fittingly bring this chapter to a close.

"By the grace of God I am now a religious and understand, maybe as yet only feebly, what it means to practice virtue in a heroic degree. I wish to assert that this servant of God had acquired such readiness, ease and facility in all virtues as to show that she possessed them in a heroic degree. I claim a right to say so, for during the years she lived in our house I never noticed the slightest defect against humility, charity, patience and temperance. I never heard her utter a word that was not necessary or useful, nor did she ever speak of her attainments, early education and wealth. In the midst of so many humiliations and suffering her courage never once failed, but she was calm and serene in soul and in her external countenance. In sickness and in desolation of spirit, worse than bodily disease, she was never heard to lament or complain. What I here state is also the opinion of many pious persons who have known our blessed Gemma."

Chapter XIV

PRAYERS, DEVOTIONS, AND DESOLATIONS

The aim of prayer is to fix the soul in a state of union with God. It winds in and out through the manifold actions, moral and otherwise, that are forever springing up in our life. Like tendrils of the vine it entwines itself around our other acts and intermingles with them. It pervades the whole soul, and through all varieties of action makes itself constantly felt. Through prayer our lives are filled with ever new floods of light and love. All saints were men of prayer. Gemma prayed not only at stated times, but she may be said to have lived on prayer; it had become the essence of her life. She realized to the full the counsel of our Lord, "Watch ye, therefore, praying at all times." Her soul remained always directed toward God and never lost sight of Him.

Only once, we are told, was this conscious realization of the Divine presence interrupted for a few minutes. Someone had given her a few accounts to make up. As they were complicated, she concentrated herself so much on them that for an instant she lost the sense of God's presence. In relating this fact. Gemma adds: "For a while I was greatly disturbed about it. I asked God to forgive me and He did so at once." One cannot help being lost in admiration at the ways of the saints. If we cannot tread the same heights let us at least humble ourselves profoundly.

Like most saints, Gemma Galgani loved to speak to Jesus in her own way. She used to join in the rosary, which was said every evening by the family, and recite that of the Seven Sorrows of our Lady. We have the testimony of Signora Cecilia that Gemma loved these prayers; that she used to take a leading part in them, called the children and in various ways coaxed them to pray. Yet, it must be confessed, she never enjoyed vocal prayer half so well as meditation.

Comparing these two forms of union with God she wrote: "It does not help me much to read prayers from books or repeat Our Fathers and Hail Marys; they do not satisfy, but only weary me, so I do the best I can." Words like these remind us of a similar passage in the autobiography of the Little Flower of Lisieux, "I have not the courage to search through books for beautiful prayers; they are so numerous that it would only make my head ache, and besides, each one is more lovely than another. Unable either to say them all or to choose between them, I do as a child would who cannot read — I say just what I want to say to God, quite simply, and He never fails to understand." Howsoever that be, the fact remains that both these saints had learned from childhood to solve every difficulty by prayer, or as St. Philip would playfully put it, "by the knees."

Besides realizing the importance of prayer, which is the breath of the soul, Gemma understood likewise the value of the Eucharist, which is the center and focus of Christian piety. Her passionate love for Jesus in the Blessed Sacrament, *Gesú Sacramentato*, as He is so expressively called in Italian, may be said to constitute the romance of her life. A moth, a butterfly, forever fluttering round and round the light of a lamp, is the image that comes up to the mind in the attempt to describe the unquenchable desire of her heart to be unceasingly near Jesus. You will remember the days of her First Communion, when at nine years of age she would say to a companion who had also made her First Communion: "I feel I am burning. I feel there is a fire kindled in my heart. Don't you feel the same?" This fire, Father Williamson remarks, once kindled, never went out; in time, it became a devouring flame so that she could write to her spiritual director:

"O Father, if you could only say in a few days' time: 'Gemma was a victim of love and died of love,' what a blessed death! Would I were dissolved; would that my heart were turned to ashes, and that all could say: 'The heart of Gemma has been consumed by Jesus.' "

With what loving care she prepared to receive Him! The night preceding Holy Communion was spent as a preparation for the morning. Her longing was so intense that she was impatient for the night to pass, so that the time for Holy Communion might come quickly. "Who will be first to seek You tomorrow morning?" she once exclaimed and replied with exquisite love and simplicity: "It will be myself."

And when the shadows of evening began to fall, and her life hastened to its close, even with a temperature at 104 degrees, this heroic girl would get up and drag herself to the church to partake of "The Bread of the Strong." In one of her ecstasies, she said:

"Jesus, listen to what my confessor asks me: 'What do you do, Gemma, whilst you are before Jesus?' What do I do? When I am with Jesus Crucified, I suffer; and when I am with Jesus in the Blessed Sacrament, I love."

Like St. Bernard she had the sweet name of Jesus ever on her lips. It had become a kind of refrain, an ejaculatory prayer to express her deep love for the Divine Savior. In her Letters and Ecstasies she repeats the name of Jesus well over 2,322 times, that is, on an average ten or twelve times in every one of her letters.

We will quote one more passage from her many impassioned addresses to our Lord:

"My Jesus, I struggle … I die … I die all because of You. Jesus, Lord of strong souls, strengthen me, purify me, make me divine. Great God, God of every sacrifice, Jesus, help me; my Redemption, God from God, come to my aid. Continually You watch over me. I thirst for You, Jesus. Do You not see how I suffer in the morning before You come to me … You, Jesus, are the flame of my heart. My Jesus. I would love You with my whole being. All you saints in heaven, lend me your hearts."

Indeed Jesus in the holy Eucharist, Jesus Crucified, especially as venerated by the people of Lucca in their precious relic of the *Volto Santo*,
formed as much a part of Gemma's life as the daily routine of duties
which filled her day, in her own home at first, and later, in the Gianninis'
household. They were things essential to her being. Not that she had
no other devotions. There was Bartolomea Capitanio whose simple and
unassuming form of sanctity she had vowed to imitate. There was St.
Gabriel, the Passionist, who more than once had called her "sister";
and her Guardian Angel with whom she prayed and played as with a
friend and a schoolmate. Above them all there was the Blessed Virgin
Mary her doubly dear "Mamma." Gemma had no other epithet for our
Lady saving that of Mother. Left an orphan from earliest years she had
learned to turn to Mary with the simplicity of a child. We do not read of
extraordinary acts of devotion or of special fasts and abstinences kept
on the eve of her feasts. The reason is not far to seek. Gemma's life was
a continuous penance and all her prayers and colloquies with Jesus were
at the same time prayers and colloquies with Mary. She passed from one
to the other, moved and lived with them as if they were inmates of the
same home. In her letters to Father Germano, in her many ecstasies, she
repeats hundreds of times the sweet name of Mary, and calls her *la mamma mia* in the same way as she repeats more than two thousand times the
beautiful name of Jesus.

One day our Lord appeared to her, it must have been shortly after the
death of her father and mother, and pointing with the finger to a little
statue on Gemma's dressing table, said: "That shall be your mother."
Gemma could not desire anything better than to have Jesus as father and
Mary as her mother.

In the meditations on the Passion of our Lord we frequently read some
of her passionate outbursts of love. "Dear Mother," she says, "how
much must have been your anguish when they crucified Him; I know
you were crucified with Him but never uttered a word of complaint.

Loving Mother, I too wish to suffer and shall never complain of my pains nor of my present state of life." Our Lady's feasts were days of special joy for Gemma. She would spend long hours meditating on her virtues, at the same time joyfully attending to the duties of the house.

"In such days," she says, "I feel more than ever the need of being with my mother and honoring her. She is so beautiful. The eternal Father has crowned her with a crown of glory and a crown of love. The jewels of this crown are her virtues ... He adorned her with the splendors of heaven; He has made her the dispenser of all His treasures, I love this mother of mine, I love her with all my heart and if that is not enough she must give me a heart that can love her more."

The Right Reverend Father Schryvers, a religious of the Holy Redeemer, in a book under the title *Ma mère*, relates the following episode which he calls delicious. One day Gemma in a vision saw herself seated on the knees of our Blessed Lady and there was resting her head on the heart of the Divine Mother. Mary turning to the girl on her knees said sweetly:

"Gemma, do you love me more than anyone else?"

"Oh, no," she replied. "I love another person more than you."

"Tell me who it is," asked Mary pressing the child to her heart.

"I must not tell you," replied the girl, wistfully looking into her eyes, and added: "Had you but come the other day, in the evening, you would have seen Him whose beauty is like yours, and whose hair is of the color of your hair."

"But tell me His name," insisted our Lady.

"It is your Son Jesus," Gemma replied with utmost affection, "so dear to me."

Then the Divine Mother pressing once more Gemma to herself, said, "Oh, yes, love Him, love Him much, love Him alone," and the vision disappeared.

The secret of Gemma's sanctity, I have no hesitation in affirming, lay in prayer and suffering. Hers was from the start a life penetrated through and through and saturated with the supernatural which had entered into the very composition of her being. Yet even the most austere asceticism is rendered easy and pleasurable so long as the individual, conscious of an omnipotent power sustaining his weakness, can bask undisturbed in the sun of divine favors. Desolation in prayer, which St. John of the Cross calls "the dark night," has been universally admitted as the acid test of the true saint.

In going through Gemma's correspondence to her spiritual director one feels as if one were reading the delightful effusions of the Canticle of Canticles, and one may wonder whether the heroine is entirely human, or whether, after all, it is not all a dream, an illusion or a merely pathological idyll. Then, all on a sudden, one comes across lines which bring one back to the realities of human existence. The writer seems to forget the sweetness of her Holy Communions. The consolations and spiritual joys of the past life sink into a lake of absolute oblivion, and she speaks of desolation and of supposed sins that render her an object of contempt before God and before men.

"The state of my soul," she says to Father Germano, "is darkness itself out of which I cannot distinguish anything. What has happened to me, and where are the visions I saw and the angelic melodies I heard in the days that are gone? It seems to me I have been dreaming a long dream which has left me tired and weary. Where is Jesus? He comes no more when I call unto Him. I seek Him in vain; He answers my questions no more. I always love Him, though I no longer feel His love."

As we go on reading we meet with passages that suggest long days of woeful temptations. The devil insinuates thoughts of despair and tells her she is a child of damnation. "Where is Jesus," she cries out, "where is He? Have mercy on me. O God. I cannot live without Jesus."

Passages like this could be multiplied as Gemma's letters are many and deal almost exclusively with the state of her soul. I close with one quotation characteristic of all others throwing a flood of light on traits of her sanctity.

"I really do not know whether I still live," she writes to Father Germano, "if I call Jesus, if I seek Him, He answers not. In the past He used to come to me, now I go to Him and call Him, but not only does He not answer me, but He sends me away. I turned to Him again, ever to be repulsed ... Of the days of my past joyful life I do not speak to you here because I remember them no more. I cannot even think of Jesus, or better, I think of Him always, but it is all so different ... What desolations I suffer in my prayer. I do not seem to like it any more. The time I spend in church is so long now and so tedious. My meditations have become to me a martyrdom, a real Purgatory. But I have not given them up. Oh, what have I come to! It cannot be worse. All the same I am happy because that is the will of God. I have shortened neither my prayers nor my meditations, nay in spite of it all I mean to increase them."[48]

Chapter XV

ECSTASIES AND OTHER DIVINE FAVORS

Supernatural ecstasy has been defined as a mental state consisting of two elements: the one interior and invisible, when the mind rivets its attention on a religious subject; the other, corporal and visible, when the activity of the senses is suspended, so that not only are external sensations incapable of influencing the soul, but considerable difficulty is experienced in awakening such sensations. Ecstasies are so numerous, and so well attested in the lives of the saints, that it is no longer possible, even for unbelievers, to ignore and brush them aside as mere fantasies or inventions. Freethinkers do not deny them nowadays; they try to explain them away.

It goes without saying that mental states, similar to the ecstatic, can be obtained by a natural disturbance of the organism, not wholly different from the disturbance caused by the action of supernatural agency. Ecstasies are, after all, mental processes that take place side by side, with the normal activities of psychical life. The agent or stimulus, that arouses them, may come from regions unexplored by sense experience, but the reaction itself is a vital function of our organism and faculties. To them it belongs, and it cannot but share in their conditions and modes of operation. We should bear in mind, nevertheless, that if there exist striking resemblances between the two kinds of responses, there are differences too, no less numerous, nor less striking.

Overlooking the deep-seated, more significant diversity, and focusing the attention upon the external similarities of the phenomena, a number of hypotheses have been advocated by persons bent on denying the possibility of divine intervention. Modern rationalists do not endeavor, like their predecessors of the eighteenth century, to reject ecstasies as grounded on deliberate deception. The theory of wholesale fraud stands condemned by the evidence of historical facts and has been thrown overboard. Similarly, the neural theory of physiological psychology, a characteristic view of early nineteenth-century thought, has been abandoned.

Somewhat different is the case of the very numerous pathological hypotheses. A number of scientists, especially among medical students, assert that ecstasy is but another form of lethargy or catalepsy; that it can be compared to somnambulism or to the reveries and disordered fancies occasioned by the use of alcohol, ether, chloroform, opium, and similar drugs. Yet such forms of impairing and paralyzing the nervous system, besides causing physical conditions of posture and movements different from those of the ecstatic, leave in their train aftereffects diametrically opposed to those of spiritual ecstasy. As Father Poulain, S.J., says, the use of narcotics has never enabled a man to lead a purer life, to better himself and others, much less to become a saint.[49]

More popular are the attempts to explain the phenomena of mysticism by their analogy to the facts of abnormal psychology. It is in clinics and laboratories, they say, that ecstasies must be cured or unmasked. Readers will remember the pitiful story of Anne Catherine Emmerich, and how shamefully she was treated by what claimed to be a Prussian civil commission of inquiry. It arrived at Dülmen on August 10, 1819. Its investigation lasted three weeks. It wanted, at all costs, to show up Anne Catherine, and make her confess that it was the French priests who were intriguing with her in order "to restore faith in legends." It ended in much harassing and manhandling of the mystic and in a quarrel of the commissioners among themselves when the nurse, Frau Vitmer, stood up to them without flinching, refusing to tell lies just to please them. Its report has disappeared. Psychological experiments were recently suggested in the case of Theresa Neumann. They have been warded off, so far, by the stanch refusal of a fond parent to lend his child for the purposes and uses of experimental clinics.[50]

To the advocates of the emotional theory, ecstasy is but a phenomenon entirely natural. The individual, they say, experiences violent emotions in consequence of which he loses the use of his senses; and as there is nothing to occupy his attention, it follows that his mind is taken up by some trifling thought, so trifling indeed, for these people, that it needs no consideration. Does emotion, even when intense and vehement, destroy sensibility? Are the contents of the ecstatic mental states as unanimously described by writers on mysticism, so trifling? With regard to autosuggestion which, even more than the theory of emotion, appeals strongly to the modern mind, it has never yielded so much as a solitary case of genuine ecstasy. Nor has the hypnosis theory, bolstered up though it be by psychoanalysts, afforded so far a better explanation of the facts. The physical conditions of posture and movement in hypnotic patients are often revolting, while they are always noble and pure in ecstasy. But here, too, the main difference lies in the higher powers of the soul. The intellect is keener, more perceptive in the ecstatic; it is weak, powerless in hypnotic trance. There is, moreover, in the latter case much narrowing of the field of consciousness, the attention being riveted, to the exclusion of all other thought, upon one single idea suggested by the controlling agent. The aftereffects are too well known to need further notice and discussion.

Yet it must be conceded that emotions play a large part in spiritual life. After all, grace, as we said on more than one occasion in this book, adapts itself to nature and operates in it, and through it, manipulating its various activities and powers for the sanctification of the soul. Indeed, after a careful study of the Autobiography and the Letters, it is clear to the present writer that our mystic was endowed with strong imagination and was by temperament easily excitable and emotional. God's grace, her continuous prayer coupled with the will to be a saint have turned these traits of character into instruments of sanctity.

Ecstasies are a distinctive feature of the biography of Gemma. Starting at an early period of her spiritual life, they increased, as years went by, in frequency, duration, and intensity. From the time of the stigmata they became an everyday occurrence, and even took place more than once during the day. Any thought of God which like a ray of light, flashed through her mind; any act of love, stronger than usual, was enough to release the senses from their ordinary function, and plunge her into ecstasy. Father Germano, a trustworthy eyewitness, tells us that no indication of bodily and mental anguish, no movement of any kind preceded or prepared the way to the phenomenon. It came all on a sudden. The blessed retained during it the posture she had at the moment immediately before the rapture. The activity of the senses alone, especially that of touch, was suspended. You could pinch, prick, or burn the skin round about her eyes without eliciting the least sensitive reaction. Apart from this, and from a celestial transfiguration of her face, there was no visible mark of the mysterious influence.

Describing the ecstasies of Gemma more in detail Father Germano distinguishes them into three classes: The lesser ecstasies, the perfect, and the extraordinary. Those of the first class were the most frequent. They occurred sometimes several times in the course of a day and were marked by a greater spontaneity and simplicity. In these, whether an infused light illumined her soul, or some heavenly vision presented itself to her gaze, the world of sense vanished all at once from before her. In an instant her whole being seemed caught up into Paradise, though she gave no indication by any bodily movement of this flight which was purely one of the spirit. Indeed one could not perceive she was in ecstasy save by looking into her sparkling eyes fixed on heaven or directed toward the vision which she saw. Father Germano had many opportunities of observing our Saint in this kind of ecstasy when they prayed or recited the Divine Office together. He would place himself at one side of the table with Gemma at the other, breviary in hand. They recited the psalms in the usual way, and read the lessons of Matins in turn, the ecstatic answering versicles and responses with wonderful exactness, and turning over the leaves of her book whenever necessary. And yet the exercise of the senses remained all the time suspended; her eyes which served her only to read were dead to every other impression. If, for any reason, they were obliged to interrupt their pious exercise, she at once resumed the use of her senses, only to lose it when taking up again the thread of the divine praises where they had broken off.

The greater ecstasies of Gemma were less frequent, but of a deeper and loftier nature. They also lasted longer, from half an hour to an hour, and in them she remained wholly insensible. They took place, as a rule, in the morning when she approached the Holy Table, or when she visited our Lord in the Blessed Sacrament exposed for the worship of the faithful during the devotion of the Forty Hours, or on other like occasions when her fervor of spirit was greater than usual.

Her extraordinary ecstasies took place twice a week, toward eight o'clock on Thursday evenings and at about three o'clock on the afternoons of Friday. They also occurred at irregular intervals in the course of the year. They generally began while she was conversing with the family during the aftermeal hours and, on feeling their approach, she used to withdraw to the privacy of her chamber.[51]

At the time of the spiritual trance the ecstatic was wont to address, or listen to the speech of, some heavenly personage — a saint, our Blessed Lord, the Virgin Mary — who visibly appeared to her. Often her discourses consisted in a hymn of praise to the majesty and power of God; at other times in a prayer, an outburst of love, a petition of graces for persons whose repentance or self-surrender she had set her heart on obtaining. Often, too, they welled forth from the inner recesses of her soul into a eulogy of a particular virtue, especially of humility and that deep sense of sinfulness, which, strange enough, is never absent from the utterances of this most innocent girl.

Yet, we should not search in these colloquies for the astounding revelations that have given a world-wide reputation to such books as *The City of God* by Maria of Agreda and *The Sorrowful Passion* of Catherine Emmerich. If Gemma's spiritual messages can be likened to those of other saints, I, for one, would rather find a comparison in the meditations and soliloquies of St. Augustine, St. Bernard, and St. Bonaventure. She, no doubt, seldom reaches the depth of these great masters of mysticism but suggests it, and summons us to prayer with their own celestial ring.

We are indebted to the foresight of Father Germano for rescuing from oblivion a large number of our Saint's conversations while in a mystic trance. Stress is deliberately laid on the word conversation or dialogue because her speeches not infrequently lack continuity; there are colons and semicolons, breaks and pauses during which the ecstatic seems to listen attentively to the apparition. When she takes up once more the thread of her ideas, it is not from the last clue, but in answer to the questioning of the vision.

One must needs fail to grasp the full import and beauty of these colloquies if one overlooks these frequent omissions and significant pauses. They link the various parts into a harmonious whole.

Unfortunately not all the speeches of Gemma have been published. In the little volume before me thirty-three are found out of a total number of one hundred and fifty collected by the late Father Germano.[52] They are the longest, the more complete outpouring of her heart on solemn occasions, in particular at the time of the stigmata, from Thursday to Friday evening. Naturally enough the question will be asked: What confidence can we place in them? What marks of authenticity do they offer? It is recognized today that the secretaries who made public the revelations of Maria of Agreda, of Catherine Emmerich, and of Marie Lataste touched them up to an extent which it is now difficult to determine. But we know that there never was in the Giannini home a formal secretary to write down the visions on little sheets of paper, the source and origin of Clement Brentano's voluminous Journal. What happened is clearly stated in a sworn declaration of the two girls responsible for the transmission of these documents to posterity.

"By the advice and command of Reverend Father Germano, C.P., Gemma's spiritual director, we have been careful to take down, for more than three years, from the lips of the Servant of God, all she said when rapt in ecstasy. This occurred often. As the holy girl lived in our house, it was easy for us to take turns in the performance of our task without her knowledge, the more so because she was at the time out of her senses. For God's glory and for the sake of truth, we hereby declare to have written what we heard during the rapture without any addition and alteration."

This valuable testimony is signed by the two girls, Cecilia and Euphemia Giannini. The latter was an intimate friend of Gemma, her confidante for whom the Blessed had no secrets. Later, as we have already pointed out, she became a nun of the Visitation and was known in religion as Sister Maria Gemma Maddalena.

We wish to lay the utmost stress upon these historical details that can never be too highly valued. They explain both the merits and short-comings of the ecstasies; their raciness and abruptness, the south-wind fragrance of their native soil, and the quaint phrase so well known to readers of the *Letters*. In his brochure, *Mystical Experience*, Louis Massignon, endeavoring to examine one by one the conditions to which the language of mystics has to submit once it finds expression, remarks:

"Their verbal reactions, deprived as they are of the normal means of expressing emotions of human source, are in their case peculiarly frustrate and awkwardly personal. The more sincere they are, the more they bear the mark of their native extraction, the strictly individual and limited sign of their early education: the Quattrocentist imagery of Saint Francoise Romaine's visions; the literary technique, borrowed from Gargilaso de la Vega, of Saint John of the Cross; the animal symbolism of Saint Francis of Sales; the poetic imagery of St. Thérèse of the Child Jesus. Despite the way in which it may jar on the artist, despite the way in which it may disappoint the philosopher, this dialect accent, this raciness of the soil, this childish recitative, is a precious testimony to the authenticity of the mystical documents which retain it."[53]

Gemma's ecstatic experiences continued to the last days of her life, but the stigmata, or at least their external manifestations, came to an end in February of 1901. Our Lord, of whom, by order of her spiritual directors, she had often asked to be free from the stigmata, was pleased to hear the prayers of His servant and to take away from her all external evidences of divine favors. Yet, as with other saints, raised by God to the highest summits of mysticism so also in the case of Gemma Galgani, we meet with the occurrence of the greatest variety of supernatural phenomena. With some of them we shall deal hereafter. There is just space enough in the last part of this chapter to speak of a few phenomena which bear greater resemblance to the ecstasies.

Gemma seems to have experienced in herself all the pains and sorrows of the sanguinary drama of Calvary. "Jesus," she used to say, "was the man of sorrows. Like Him I must be a daughter of pain and suffering." On several occasions, in imitation of our Lord in the garden of Gethsemane, she too experienced the sweat of blood. The blasphemies that were uttered at home and the knowledge she had of the sins committed by persons known to her, were enough to cause a sweat of blood. Often it trickled down from all the pores of her skin, staining the clothes. At times, we are told, it flowed visibly to the outer garments. This phenomenon occurred frequently during the year 1901, in which year Gemma longed to be a victim for sinners. She was heard to say in the ecstasies of this period, "Jesus, revenge Yourself on me, but save all the sinners." The sweat of blood happened even more frequently in August of this same year as she had taken upon herself to atone for the negligences and the sins of priests.

The crown of thorns, too, must here be mentioned as one of Gemma's mystical experiences. She speaks of it for the first time in her diary under the date of July 9, 1900. "This evening," she says, "after six days of spiritual desolation, I was able to find Jesus again in meditation. I began my prayer, as I usually do every Thursday ... It was on the Passion of our Divine Savior." Here follows a long description of the crowning of thorns which had happened to her in the ecstasy, and she adds: "On the following day, July 20, at three o'clock in the afternoon, I went to pray. Jesus appeared to me, removed the crown of thorns from my head and placed it on His own. All pain, I had suffered from Thursday evening suddenly ceased." These phenomena were witnessed by several persons who have attested them in their depositions on the occasion of the processes for Gemma's beatification. Mother Gemma Giannini, the most authentic and authoritative witness, gives a minute description of the coronation and says: "The phenomenon began on Thursday evening at the usual hour and ended at about four or five o'clock in the afternoon of Friday. It also occurred on the three subsequent Thursdays."

Indeed the story of this holy girl, chiefly during the last four years of her life, reads like the romance of a martyr who rejoices in his afflictions and his agonies.

"Father," Gemma writes to the spiritual director, "Father, today is Thursday! How glad I feel to spend an hour in company with the suffering Jesus. When Thursday evening comes I am wholly changed, I feel so happy, and Friday is always for me a feast day."

Putting together the dates of the various documents at our disposal we find that these phenomena, to which the scourging must be added, were suffered by Gemma throughout the latter part of her life, but they seem to have occurred more frequently during the year 1901, as appears from the attestations of witnesses which mostly refer to this time.

"O Jesus," says Gemma in one of these Passiontide ecstasies, "O Jesus, what has happened to Thee? Thy holy person has become the mockery and laughing stock of all. They all blaspheme my Jesus, they mock and laugh at Him, they make Him suffer so much. Oh, if I could, Jesus, with my blood ... yes with my blood I wish I could cleanse all the places where sinners offend Thee. How powerful was love in Thy heart. What are they doing, those sinners, to Thee, O Jesus? Do they never tire of striking and paining Thee? Let them stop those blows on Thee ... Thou dost not deserve them, but I yes ... not Thou. It is I who have sinned. Thou art innocent, but I, I am full of sins. Tonight, Jesus, I alone wish to suffer or, if Thou wiliest it, we shall suffer in company. We shall become one victim ... art Thou pleased, Jesus? Give me strength, Jesus, I ask nothing else. Dear Jesus! how many blows, dear Jesus! They go on beating Him but He can bear so patiently. Beat Him no more, do not beat Jesus but beat me. Why do you revenge yourselves on Him? Yes, revenge yourselves on me. Yes, more blows on me, Jesus, more blows. Oh God! Jesus, help me in this hour. To whom Jesus, shall I have recourse?"[54]

And the blows were falling on the poor martyr, blows so hard that the blood was flowing, big wounds were noted on her arms, on her legs and those who were present feared she might die under the pain.

Chapter XVI

THE GUARDIAN ANGEL

The teaching of the Church as regards the guardian angels is based on Scripture, tradition, and theological reasoning. Our Blessed Lord says: "See that you despise not one of these little ones: for I say unto you that their angels in heaven always see the face of My Father who is in heaven."[55] And St. Paul: "Are they not all ministering spirits, sent to minister for them who shall receive the inheritance of salvation?"[56] Many understand the following passage from the Psalms in a secondary sense of man, primarily, of course, of Christ: "He has given His angels watch over thee, that they guard thee in all thy ways."[57] "It is most suitable," says St. Bonaventure. "that fallen man should be entrusted to angelic care, and that angels should be deputed to guide and direct them. God's power, God's wisdom, and God's mercy demand it."[58]

It is, moreover, generally held that guardian angels are given to societies as well as to individuals. St. Michael, whom Daniel calls the Prince of the Synagogue, is honored by the Church in the Office of his feast as the patron and guardian of the Christian world. Nay, every religious order, every nation and kingdom is supposed to enjoy the protection of a special guardian angel. "All corporal substances," says St. Thomas, "are ruled by angels, and this is the belief not of Christian divines alone, but even pagan philosophers."

Cardinal Newman's notion of the angels before he became a Catholic will be read with interest: "It was, I suppose, to the Alexandrian school and to the early Church that I owe in particular what I definitely held about the angels. I viewed them not only as the ministers employed by the Creator in the Jewish and Christian dispensations as we find on the face of Scripture, but as carrying on, as the Scripture also implies, the economy of the visible world. I considered them as the real causes of motion, life, and light, and of those elementary principles of the physical universe, which, when offered in their developments to our senses, suggest to us the notion of cause and effect, and of what are called the laws of nature. This doctrine I have drawn out in a sermon for Michaelmas Day, written in 1831. I say of the angels: Every breath of air, and ray of light and heat, every beautiful prospect is, as it were, the skirts of their garments, the waving of the robes of those whose faces see God."[59]

It is hard to find anywhere in sacred or profane literature a more touching episode than that contained in the books of the Old Testament wherein we are told of the familiarity of Tobias with Raphael, "one of the seven Angels, which present the prayers of the saints, and go in before the glory of the Holy One." He accompanied him on his journey to Tebatana and back; he made his father see the light of heaven, and as young Tobias said, "We are filled with all good things through him."

Among the Christian saints, there are pleasing references to the guardian angels in the Acts of the Martyrs authentically drawn up by witnesses, confirmed by contemporaries and authorized by the Church which recommends them to be publicly read in solemn assemblies of the faithful. The cruel tragedies of the two holy virgins Cecilia and Agnes are turned into scenes of beauty as we become conscious of a celestial presence. In the legends of St. Peter Celestine, pope of the thirteenth century, we read how angels assisted him in building a church and how, when he offered the holy Sacrifice, unseen bells rang peals of surpassing sweetness while celestial music filled the sanctuary and the church. Even more wonderful is the story of St. Frances of Rome, one of the greatest mystics of the fifteenth century. Not only was she allowed to enjoy the sight of her angel, but had him as a companion and friend visibly by her side.

Perhaps no other saint has come nearer to St. Frances of Rome as regards intimacy of friendship with the guardian angel than Gemma Galgani. From the earliest days of her life she was enveloped in his splendor and lived in the atmosphere of his companionship, which kept her away from terrestrial attractions. She saw him with her eyes, held him by the hand, and conversed with him as if he were a human being and most intimate friend. Contemplatives require an enlightenment which raises their spiritual faculties above natural limits. "This enlightenment," says St. Thomas, "God communicates through the medium of the Guardian Angel, who, by his direction and his incessant assistance, upholds the weakness of the human spirit and makes it capable of bearing the dazzling beams of this enlightenment and its effects."[60]

It is in the fitness of things that one so raised to mystical elevations and accustomed to visions of celestial beings should need the assistance and special protection of an immortal spirit. Gemma herself describes in the autobiography what place the Guardian Angel held in the spiritual molding of her soul. "Jesus," she says, "makes my guardian angel stay with me always." There is one point worthy of note in their intimate intercourse. It was entirely subordinate to the directions of the ghostly father. The angel intervened only in his quality of mentor and left to the Church the ordinary guidance of Gemma's soul. It is indeed a recognized principle of mystical science that no one, however perfect, can be exempted from the providential law of direction; that it is for the spiritual director to pronounce in the last resort as to the divine, natural, or diabolical character of the states of soul of those whom it is his mission to direct. Gemma, on her part, ceased to have recourse to her angel and to use him as a deliverer of her messages, when obedience bade her to do so.

Father Germano had been deeply impressed, and for a while perturbed, by the descriptions she had sent him of her familiar conversations with the heavenly companion. Brought up in a more conventional school of sanctity, he thought it all a little trifling. To him these mystical familiarities lacked the dignity which we, average mortals, naturally associate with human approaches to the divine. Gemma's behavior bordered upon irreverence. Saints, like other folk, need at times to be managed, he thought, and in a letter he warned his penitent to be more worshipful, more guarded, and respectful, lest the angel should take offense and come no more. It was all well-meant, and prudent from our dull, dim-sighted perception of heavenly things. But saints have received a larger share of freedom in God's household, where they meet with celestial beings unfettered by the laws and conventions of our social intercourse. They are children of the Lord, and must play the game in their own way, or not play it at all.

Nevertheless, Gemma obeyed and wrote: "You are quite right. Father, I will not do so again. From today I will show him greater respect." And she kept her word so long as the spiritual veto lasted. On meeting the angel she said with childlike simplicity:

"Dear angel, you must bear up patiently with me, the Father does not like it and wishes me to change my manner. But listen, if at times, I seem a little rude, do not be angry. I do want to be grateful."

One morning Gemma was paying a visit to the Mantellate; she loved the nuns, their seclusion, their prayer, and would gladly have joined them in the Convent. One of the Sisters, not noticing her little companion, said:

"Gemma, you come alone?"

"No, I have my sister and another person."

"Who is that?"

"My guardian angel."

"But I do not see him."

"He is here beside me, and I see him."

On another occasion she had been fervently praying to her angel for protection. "Yes," he replied. "I shall be your guide and inseparable companion. Do you know who committed you to my keeping? It is the merciful Jesus." At these words the affectionate girl could no longer check the feelings of her heart and fell into an ecstasy together with the angel. "We both," she writes to Father Germano. "remained with Jesus. Oh, if you had been with us. Father! To be with Jesus is like plunging into the immense ocean of the divinity and grasping its deep ineffable mysteries."

Sometimes Gemma saw the angel hovering in the air with outspread wings and hands extended upon her, or he would kneel beside her and pray. If they happened to be reciting vocal prayers, such as the Rosary or the Psalms, they said them alternately as Catholics do when they meet in church. It happened, on occasions, that Gemma, with the angel close by her side, would say ejaculatory aspirations, those brief outpourings of love similar in spiritual effect to the thrust of a javelin, whence their name of ejaculations. Like two children at play, they would at once rival one another as to who would say *Viva Gesù*, using Gemma's own words, with greater fervor, and Jesus showed that He was pleased.

But the principal function of the angel was to help the mystic girl in her mental prayer and meditation. He flooded her soul with the dazzling radiance of supernatural light and set her heart afire with love for Christ, especially for the suffering Jesus of the *Volto Santo*. At any hour, in the midst of any occupation, at table or during a walk. Gemma would place herself in the presence of her heavenly guide. As in the case of St. Catherine Emmerich she could say: "The angel calls me and leads me to various places ... When he comes to me, generally I first see a light, and then his luminous form emerges from the surrounding darkness just as when, at night, you open a dark lantern ... He walks in front of me, sometimes beside me." We have it on the authority of Father Germano that no outward sign of any kind revealed the Angel's presence; except that sometimes she was rapt out of her senses and, with her large radiant eyes fixed on the object before her, became wholly unconscious to all things of sense.

In a private audience which Pope Pius X gave to Father Germano shortly after the publication of the life of Gemma Galgani, he is reported to have turned with a smile to the learned author, and said:

"Are all the marvels you tell us really true?"

"They are but a particle, a small portion," replied the Father, "of what has actually taken place."

In asking the question, His Holiness had evidently in mind the episode of the so-called "angelic letters." At any rate, it is in connection with such letters that Sister Gesualda has recorded this bit of papal conversation. And truly the angelic letters add a new chapter to the history of mysticism. Nothing similar, as far as we know, can be found in the legends of the saints, nothing so intensely human, so affectionate and beautiful. There is just one incident in the life of St. Camillo de Lellis which, we surmise, had not been forgotten by the Angel of Gemma. And why should it? There can be sport in heaven as there is beauty, truth, and love.

On July 5, 1613, a nephew of St. Camillo, one Alexander de Lellis, had gone with a score of laborers to a spot where, believing in the words of an impostor, he expected to dig out a hidden treasure. You could hear a stir among the crowd that had gathered in the public square of Bucchianico, the scene of the gold-hunting expedition. Signor de Lellis and his men were advancing armed with spades and pickaxes to start work. Of a sudden, he was seen to stop and they beheld him looking at a letter that had come into his hands from he did not know where. It was from his venerable uncle, commanding him to desist from an enterprise which could only bring ridicule upon him and his family. The letter had traveled all the way from Genoa, where the Saint lived, and had apparently been written that very morning, being dated July 5, 1613. The event was indeed miraculous and the work of an angel for, at that time, a letter from Genoa could not ordinarily reach Bucchianico in less than ten days. Naturally enough, it put an end to the quest for the hidden treasure.

Gemma's intercourse with her angel was so intimate that she often entrusted messages to him or errands. She was an orphan in the house of strangers and, owing to her extraordinary experiences, she needed someone in whom to confide the secrets of her soul. Why not start a regular correspondence with her spiritual director? Other saints had done so before. But she was poor and had no money to buy stamps with. Would not the angel, who all but played marbles with her, take charge of these letters? Well, in her innate simplicity she opened her heart, and told him of a very pressing message she had for Father Germano. No sooner said than done. The Father was then in Rome. One evening he finds an unstamped letter on his desk coming all the way from Lucca, and nobody could tell how it had come.

We should not imagine that all letters of Gemma were carried by invisible hands to their destination. Miracles are not wrought to human orders. But the fact remains that none of the letters, which under God's inspiration she handed over to her angel, failed to reach its addressee.

When the thing became known, it caused both a sensation and a great deal of opposition. People do not easily accept miracles. Perhaps Hume's objection that it is contrary to experience for miracles to be true, but that it is not contrary to experience for testimony to be false cannot altogether be despised. It has some force so long as the evidence of the miracle is not fully established. In any case someone — his name is not mentioned by any of the biographers, though we believe we could venture a guess — led by curiosity or by the prevailing scientific spirit of inquiry, undertook to hide a letter addressed to her director, and then waited for results. No miracle occurred; the angel ignored the letter which remained all the time in its hiding place. Of course it occasioned much backstairs talk among persons in the inner circle. Poor Gemma became an object of suspicion. Was it imposture? Did she buy stamps secretly or, worse still, was she under the influence of the evil spirit? Signora Cecilia in particular and Monsignor Tei, a learned priest who lived in the house, were much put out and alarmed. Were they sheltering an ally of Satan? That could not be for Gemma was too good. To the priest one thing was clear. He would take the matter in hand and commanded Gemma to send her letters in the ordinary way until, at least, God's will became better known to them all. "If it is the devil that delivers my letters," Gemma wrote to Father Germano. "you will surely recognize him. Tell me that it is he and I shall not send such letters anymore."

In the silence and solitude of his convent, amid studies and prayers, Father Germano, too, was turning fervently to God for light. Yes, might it not be Satan? Such tricks do not lie beyond the power which, as Scripture, theology, and history testify, he still retains over men. Not only did he pray to receive light and guidance, but remembering he was God's appointed director, he confidently asked for a sign. If it be Your work, O Lord, he said, let the letters come to me so that I may recognize the presence of Your finger. Meanwhile he wrote to his penitent not to send through the angels the messages intended for him, but to hand them over to Signora Cecilia. He also instructed that good lady to hide those letters carefully under lock and key, and to breathe not a word of this arrangement to Gemma. Thus the whole affair was to pass entirely in God's own hands.

On June 21, 1901, Gemma wished to send an angelic letter to her director, but obedient to orders received, she gave the letter to her good "mamma" and went cheerfully on with her customary household duties. The letter, for greater security, was passed on to Father Agrimonti who was in the secret and could be trusted for the safekeeping of it. In the afternoon of the following day Gemma was in the garden looking after the smallest child of the Gianninis, when she saw the angel passing with a letter in his hands. She turned immediately to Signora Cecilia nearby to tell her of the vision. Needless to say a feeling of curiosity, strong in women at all times but on this occasion irresistible, prompted an immediate search for the letter which, indeed, had disappeared and safely gone to its destination.

We shall close this chapter with one more instance culled from the many that are reported as regards these angelic letters. On the day after this event, June 22, 1901, Gemma wrote two letters, one for Father Germano and the other for Reverend Mother M. Giuseppa, a Passionist of Corneto. She placed them in the same envelope and prayed her angel to deliver them to the persons for whom they were intended. We surmise, though we find it nowhere stated, that Gemma's recourse to the guardian angel can be explained in part by the fact that she did not always know the address of Father Germano, who, as a preacher of great repute, had to travel to various towns and provinces of Italy. Be that as it may, according to the orders of her director she gave the two letters to Signora Cecilia. The closed envelope was once more concealed in the room of Father Agrimonti and placed between two holy pictures, one of St. Gabriel and the other of St. Paul of the Cross.

On the following day Gemma once more informed Signora Cecilia that she had seen the angel with the letters, which had in fact disappeared from their hiding place. Father Germano received both letters at Corneto, where he was staying at the time. The sign he had asked from God was that he wished to receive one letter at least directly from the hands of the angel. Father Germano himself never spoke of the way the two letters came to him. But the Superior of the Passionists at Corneto was wont to narrate how, late in the evening, one day a young man had arrived asking to be introduced to the room of Father Germano, for whom he had an urgent message. Did the holy director recognize an angel in the unknown visitor? We know not, but it remains true that from that day he no longer entertained any doubt about the angelic letters and gave full permission to Gemma to send them in her own way, whenever God inspired her to do so.

Chapter XVII

CHIAPPINO

It is well known that God permits even His chosen ones to suffer the assaults of Satan. In reading about his wiles and his persecutions of Gemma one is irresistibly reminded of a chapter in the life of St. John Marie Vianney, the famous Curé d'Ars. Curiously enough by a coincidence of what the French would describe as *espieglerie*, both saints applied a nickname to their archenemy. The Curé d'Ars spoke of the evil one as "Grappin," whilst Gemma called him "Chiappino." Both terms express in the characteristic language of the people the main function of the devil. In popular theology he is principally a robber of souls, a grappin or chiappino, an idea contained in the graphic metaphor of St. Peter. "Your adversary, the devil, goes about like a roaring lion, seeking whom he may devour."[61]

Indeed, moral life would not be half so irksome, nor such a continuous warfare, but for the wiles and temptations of the evil spirit. Not all the fallacies of Freudian psychoanalysis will ever succeed in explaining the facts of temptation in a way different from the teaching of the Church and the conclusions of universal experience. Doubtless the world and the flesh must be reckoned among the enemies to be guarded against, but they are rendered more formidable owing to the devil's persevering activity in seeking to compass the ruin of the soul. Unfortunately he has persuaded a large number of people to believe that he does not exist, or if he does, that he troubles himself little about them. It is his clever-est ruse in which he is helped by men of learning. This new doctrine is largely an agnostic attempt to find in psychology a complete answer to the old conflict between the law of the mind and that of the members, between the good that one wills and the evil that one does. St. Paul knew and spoke of it: "Unhappy man that I am, who shall deliver me from the body of this death? The grace of God by Jesus Christ our Lord." But these people will have little to do with Christ; they tell us that our earthly life is a final state, which alone it is man's duty to perfect; sin and the devil are subjective fears, probably of an acquired type, passed into instincts through generations of half-civilized ancestors.

The teaching of the Church as regards these truths is known to ev-ery Catholic child that has gone through the rudiments of the penny catechism. They may be ignorant of the reasons for believing in their faith, but they hold it, and feel a sense of security which modern elabo-rate theories of religion cannot give. It is a pity that quite a number of persons seem to suffer from a sort of modernity complex, and, in mat-ters of such vital importance, are easily led astray by most extravagant opinions if only these opinions are presented in the name and language of science.

Holy Scripture is full of references to the spirit of darkness bent on waging war against God and His creature. In the opening chapters of Genesis he appears as the tempter of our First Parents. Christ says of him that he was a murderer from the beginning.[62] "The wicked," says St. Luke, "shall go into everlasting fire which was prepared for the devil and his angels."[63] "For our wrestling is not against flesh and blood, but against principalities and powers, against the rulers of the world of this darkness, against the spirits of wickedness in the high places."[64] Basing their conclusions on these and similar passages of Holy Scripture, and on the teaching of the Fathers from the earliest centuries, theologians tell us that Satan attacks man because of the perversity of his nature. Good men do good things from the kindness of their nature. Now no men were ever so naturally disposed to be kind as the angels were. It follows that when the angelic nature was perverted it, so to say, reversed itself and became essentially disposed to desire and to effect evil. Secondly, the devil hates man, because of God's image impressed on his soul. Lastly, because of the love of God and of Jesus Christ for man, he hates man with a demon's hatred. I may be pardoned for quoting Milton's beautiful description of the hatred of Satan for God and man:

What though the field be lost?
All is not lost: the unconquerable will,
And study of revenge, immortal hate,
And courage never to submit or yield.

* * *

Here we may reign secure, and, in my choice
To reign is worth ambition, though in hell:
Better to reign in hell than serve in heaven.

* * *

So spoke the apostate angel, though in pain,
Vaunting aloud, but racked with deep despair.[65]

Said the Angel to Tobias: "And because thou wast acceptable to God, it was necessary that temptation should prove thee."[66] It is a rule of sanctity to which Gemma, perhaps in a more striking degree than other saints, was subject. In a letter to Father Germano, she says:

During the last two days Jesus has been telling me after Holy Communion: "My daughter, the devil will wage against you a great war." These words I hear in my heart continuously. Please pray for me ... Who will win this battle: the devil or my soul? How sad this thing makes me! Where will the war come from? I am forever thinking about it instead of praying Jesus to give me strength and help. I have told you in time and now I leave this matter to you that you may help me.

Your poor Gemma[67]

The attack was not long delayed. Indeed the devil seems to have divined Gemma's future sanctity at an early period of her life.

"When she was still living at her house," writes Signora Cecilia, "devils used to hide themselves in her room taking the shape of dogs, cats, and monkeys, sometimes of wild ugly men. They tormented her in all possible ways beating her with ropes. She was very young and spoke of this thing to her confessor who sent for me suggesting that I should make investigations into the matter."

At the time of the above-quoted letter the demon began his assaults with a series of temptations of lust and impurity. She had been so innocent as hardly to have any knowledge of the sins of the flesh, yet the prince of darkness contrived to fill her mind with strange fancies, and filthy imaginings. Indeed the horrified child endured tortures in these attacks. Like St. Paul in his hour of trial, she would passionately turn to Jesus to have mercy and spare her those ugly thoughts, or, if that could not be, at least to change them into any other kind of suffering. But they lasted often for many days without abating one jot or one tittle. In the end she always emerged from the struggle victorious, but the devil would give no respite. There had been reverses of fortune in her family such as the loss of parents, of property, and dear friends. She was lonely, at times afflicted by illnesses that came and disappeared in a strange way; she had enemies even among those whose assistance seemed to be indispensable to her very existence. What a rare opportunity for the fiend to renew the assault. He was not slow to make the most of it and, when he found her spiritually depressed, returned to the charge cunningly suggesting that all her prayers and devotions were of no avail; that she was deceived and had no chance of salvation. This kind of warfare continued almost throughout Gemma's life, and was all the more trying for being accompanied by the suspicions of various persons about her supernatural experiences. The temptations to gluttony to which St. Margaret Mary was subjected are comparatively rare; the commonest are those of lust, despair, and blasphemy. It is painful to read the account Gemma gives to the director of her long, uninterrupted efforts against the insinuations of the evil spirit that God had abandoned her: that she was forever doomed, a child of perdition. "Don't you see," the tempter would whisper to her ears, "that this Jesus does not hear you, and that He will have nothing to do with you?" One day the confessor had asked her to pray for some sinners and she promised to do so. Soon after returning home the devil, whom she at once recognized, told her: "You may pray as much as you like for your soul, but leave the sinners alone, or you will pay for it."[68]

Satan did not seem satisfied with harassing his victim by common trials and temptations. He had recourse to visions and apparitions. Such intervention of the devil is far from being so rare as some might think. It is often met with on the contrary, in the lives of the saints and is mentioned among the signs of mystical favors. St. Antony of the Desert, St. Benedict, St. Hilarion, St. Francis of Assisi, St. Teresa to whom the devil appeared as a little Negro that pulled her about in many ways, St. Catherine of Siena, St. Mary Magdalen of Pazzi, Blessed Angela of Foligno, the saintly Curé d'Ars, and others are famous examples of it. All have had to submit more or less to obsessions of the devil.

To Gemma he would often appear either in the guise of a ferocious dog, of some hideous monster or of a giant infuriated with rage. In one of her letters she writes:

"Yesterday as usual I passed a very bad night. The devil came before me in the form of a gigantic man, very big and very tall, who kept on beating me all night and repeating: 'For you there is no hope of salvation. You belong to me.' I answered that God was very merciful and therefore I feared nothing. At this he was so enraged that he struck me a heavy blow on the head exclaiming: 'May you be cursed,' and disappeared. I went to my room to rest a little. He was there again and again beat me with a knotted rope, and asked whether I would let him teach me to do evil. I answered, 'No.' then he struck me more violently and began beating my head on the ground. At a certain point I cried out, 'Eternal Father, through the most precious Blood of Jesus deliver me.' I do not quite know what happened then, but the devil thrust me from the bed so that my head struck the ground with great violence. I felt a great pain, became unconscious and remained there on the ground till I came to my senses some time afterwards."

On another occasion she wrote: "Come quickly, Father, or at least make the exorcism from a distance. The devil has pursued me in every possible way. Ah, if you knew how I have suffered! How pleased he was this night. He seized me by the hair and dragged me about exclaiming, 'Disobedience, disobedience, now there is no more time to begin again. Come, come with me,' and he tried to carry me off to hell. He tormented me like this for more than four hours, and thus I passed the night."[69]

One day the fiend entered Gemma's room while she was writing a letter to Father Germano. He snatched the pen from her hand, tore the paper into shreds, dragged her by the hair causing her many injuries, and left shouting: "War, war against your Father, war as long as he lives." On another occasion the evil one sat in the confessional just when he knew she would present herself for the weekly confession. Gemma knelt at her place as usual, and made the sign of the Cross. Scarcely had she begun to say a few words when the tempter broke forth into a torrent of vile abuse. Trembling with fear she ran away crying, "Jesus, help me; Jesus, my Jesus, help me."

The story of the so-called devil manuscript is almost incredible. By order of Father Germano, Gemma had written a diary giving to him an account of her conscience as well as a description of her mystical experiences. This manuscript, or autobiography of Gemma's early life, written by order of the above-mentioned Father, had been handed over to Signora Cecilia, who had made all arrangements to send it by post, but one day the devil carried it away by force. It was returned after some time, the demon having been compelled by the prayers and many exorcisms of Father Germano to restore it. Here is how Gemma narrates the fact:

"One night, I do not well remember the date, I was quietly sleeping when Satan came to tempt me. For nearly an hour I fought, praying fervently and making signs of the Cross ... Then suddenly with an ejaculation to the Immaculate Conception I found myself free from the temptation. The defeated enemy longing for revenge tried to strike me, but he was not allowed to do so. 'War, war,' he shouted, 'the manuscript is in my hands,' and vanished."

The returned diary, with its pages singed and partially burned, as it came from the hands of the devil, is even to this day preserved in the "Postulazione Generale" of the Passionist Fathers in Rome.[70]

A postal card signed G. V. V., that is Giovanni Volpi Vescovo, was brought one day to the house of the Gianninis.

It was addressed to the Reverend Father Pietro-Paolo, Provincial of the Passionists, and read:

> As it will be impossible for me to see you before I leave, I would request you to have nothing to do in the foolish affair of Gemma as I have come to know from Jesus, that what has happened to her is entirely due to diabolic tricks. You should no longer interest yourself in her behalf, and should advise Father Germano to act in the same manner. If you both continue to help her, you will run the risk of causing her spiritual ruin. She does not need your assistance. I am myself sufficiently enlightened about her deceived soul. If she follows the counsels I have given her, she may yet find her way to God.
>
> A friend greets you.

Referring to this fact Gemma writes to Father Germano: "During these days 'Chiappino' has been up to all sorts of mischief. You have heard about the post-card and all the rest."[71]

Monsignor Volpi repudiated the authorship of the letter, the very style of which was of itself sufficient to indicate a more unfriendly origin.

On his part, the good Father Provincial thought the best he could do in the circumstances was to ignore it all. Would the affair stop at that? It did not, for a few days later the same Father Provincial, who had scarcely overcome the previous shock, was surprised to find that one out of three letters he had just written and had laid aside to post at a convenient time had disappeared. It dealt with some affairs of administration and contained a few references to Gemma. It was addressed to Father Germano. Nobody in the house knew anything about it. On the following day a letter was found in his room intended for him and signed by Father Germano. It ran thus:

> At about one o'clock yesterday, I received through my guardian angel the letter you wished to send me by post. I will reply at once.
>
> I wish, dear Father, we could do things twice .... Having prayed to our Venerable (St. Gabriel had not yet been canonized), he finally made me understand that Gemma is deceived. My dear Father, let us avoid further mistakes. We should not busy ourselves about the affairs of others lest we run the risk of eternal damnation. Unsay all you have said about Gemma. It were useless even to try to unmask her. All that has happened to her is mere hypocrisy and deceit. She is within the power of the devil and all our efforts will be of no avail. Let us keep clear of this business.
>
> The esteem I had for her in the past, has now changed into hatred and disgust. I wish you could feel in the same way. For my part I shall never speak nor write again about that hypocrite. Yesterday's trick was of her own doing; she hid the letter which my angel picked up and brought to me.
>
> I am more concerned about the Signora Cecilia. You had better warn her to send Gemma away from the house before all its people are ruined forever. The Venerable Gabriel has dictated this letter.

That other letter concealed in a drawer (presumably the one hidden between two holy pictures) was not brought by her angel, but Gemma herself sent it by post after taking the money from the house. I have ceased to believe in any of these things. You may warn her once more, and then have nothing more to do with her affairs.

It is necessary to inform the Gianninis about the warnings of our Venerable in order that they may send her away. I might add much more, but I hope you have understood. The best is to refer the matter to the Bishop and deprive her of Holy Communion.

Germano.

On receipt of such extraordinary correspondence the Father Provincial was simply staggered. It came to him as a shock. "Either someone," he wrote afterwards, "was trying to fool me or the devil had a finger in it." — However that may be, there was more trouble to come. One morning all the letters of Father Germano to Gemma, which were in the keeping of Signora Cecilia, were found scattered all over the house. Who had done it? This event happening as it did, soon after the arrival of the suspicious postal card and of the letter of Father Provincial, cast a heavy cloud around our Saint. Unwilling definitely to lay the guilt upon her, the people of the house could not help feeling uneasy at what they had at least reason to attribute to her capricious behavior.

To understand Gemma's state of mind while these things were taking place one should visualize the scene in its proper setting — the suspicions of the Gianninis, the insinuations and adverse criticism of many people, her own loneliness, her uncertainties and the inability to say or to prove anything. No wonder that she writes an anxious letter to Father Germano:

"Jesus is yet exposed on the altar. Please, Father, go and ask Him who has scattered all your letters to me about the house ... I am under suspicion, but I don't think I have done it ... They all behave strangely toward me ... Do you see it. Father? All your letters were found thrown hither and thither about the house ... Jesus will explain the matter to you. I spoke of it to the confessor who assures me it is the devil. What will he be up to next?"

To the events already narrated — and still more are found in the letters and autobiography — Father Germano adds a personal experience of his own which occurred one night, when Gemma was dangerously ill. He had gone over to assist her and was saying his Breviary in a corner of the room when he saw a large, dark cat entering and tearing round and round the room. It sprang upon the end of the iron bedstead directly in front of the sick girl, staring at her with eyes like two burning coals. "What is the matter?" said the Father, not without some agitation. Gemma replied: "My Father, don't be afraid, it is this hateful demon who wants to annoy me, but fear him not, he will not harm you." The good Father sprinkled some holy water upon the bed and the vision vanished, leaving the sick girl tranquil as if nothing had happened.

It is not easy to give a satisfactory explanation of these very startling and disconcerting phenomena. We read in Job[72] that on a certain day when the sons of God came to stand before the Lord, Satan also was present among them. Commenting on this line and on the whole story of Job's temptations Bishop Challoner writes:

"This passage represents to us in a figure, accommodated to the ways and understandings of men: (1) the restless endeavors of Satan against the servants of God; (2) that he can do nothing without God's permission; (3) that God does not permit him to tempt them above their strength: but assists them by His Divine grace in such a manner, that the vain efforts of the enemy only serve to illustrate their virtue and increase their merit."

St. Augustine, in a well-known metaphor, compares the devil to a dog chained to a post from which it can indeed bark but cannot bite, unless a person voluntarily puts himself within the sphere of his power. Gemma herself heard our Lord saying: "Be sure, in My cross there is salvation.

The devil has no real power against those souls that suffer for My sake. My daughter, many would have been lost had I not crucified them."

Chapter XVIII

THE PASSIONIST NUNS AT LUCCA

Although never a cloistered nun Gemma Galgani has been rightly regarded as a spiritual daughter of St. Paul of the Cross, the founder of the religious Congregation of the Passionists. Her association with them dates back to the time of the mysterious sickness and of its subsequent miraculous cure. Did not St. Gabriel alight from heaven to call her "Sister," and to place the badge of his Order upon her heart? When, on the occasion of the Jubilee Mission in Lucca she told Father Gaetano her long cherished desire of becoming a religious, he had remarked: "There are Passionist nuns." These casual words, coupled with the frequent apparitions of St. Gabriel, could not but give a definite direction to her vocation at the time of her perplexities as regards the choice of the convent best suited to her calling. Henceforward she will no longer doubt that her place lies among the Passionist nuns. If the rule of the Visitation had seemed too mild, that of the Passionists, prayerful, austere, and well known for its characteristic love of the sufferings of Christ, offered genuine attractions to her mystical soul. It is true that under the guidance of the confessor, and because of repeated refusals from the nuns of Corneto — in spite of the exertions of Father Provincial in her behalf — she was to knock at the door of other religious institutions. Yet deep in her heart there lurked the certainty that God wished her to be a Passionist. That these aspirations were never fulfilled; that the dream of her life remained but a dream;

that she would die a Passionist in spirit, not in reality, constitutes one of those problems of Divine Providence, so conspicuous in the life of St. Gemma Galgani, to which we bow in faith and humility, for they are hidden behind a veil too impenetrable to our sight.

One day, having heard that there was a rumor abroad of founding a convent of Passionist nuns in Lucca, she became greatly interested in the project, and thought of asking St. Gabriel about it.

"Will the convent really be founded?" she asked him.

"Not for another two years," he replied, but at the same time he assured her that his words would come true. To the further query whether she might be a Passionist, he answered:

"You will be my sister."

"But where? Must I go to Corneto?"[73]

"Why go so far?"

"To forget all and be forgotten by all," was Gemma's naive reply. St. Gabriel did not answer, but blessed her and disappeared.

In relating this vision to Father Germano, she added: "Help me to become a Passionist, my will is resolute; do help me, I cannot wait any longer, I have nothing, I am very poor, but I have an intense desire to be a Passionist." In another letter to the same Father she says:

"A short time ago a Passionist Father told me that in October the Passionist nuns open their novitiate. Can I hope that the lowest place there may be for the humblest daughter of St. Paul? I will be good and obedient. Tell the nuns that if they will have me, I shall be their servant. I can sweep, wash dishes, draw water and do needlework ... If you knew how much I suffer by not being a Passionist. ... Jesus consoles me, and says, 'there is a life even more blessed than that of the convent.' Do you know what that life is? My guardian angel has not told me. Indeed, I have nothing to complain of at present, but how better would I be in a convent where I could love Jesus and suffer much for His sake; best of all how happy I should be to go to heaven. The confessor does not allow me to ask for this last grace; if he were but to permit me to ask, Jesus would take me to Himself. How glad that consent would make me for I cannot any longer live separated from Jesus, I am so much afraid of offending Him."

The consolation given her by Jesus because she could not be a Passionist seems to have been repeated, for in another letter she says: "The other morning, after Holy Communion, I asked Jesus to send me into a convent (it is the first grace I always ask of Him), and He answered: 'My daughter, there is a life more blessed than that in a convent,' and added no more. I have asked myself often what this life can be, but I have not been able to find it out, though I desire it and think of it always. When I ask Jesus to grant me that blessed life, He tells me to ask the permission of my confessor."

Thus our Lord was little by little revealing to His servant that the convent destined for her was not of this world. The idea of her religious vocation, and that of an establishment of Passionist nuns in Lucca, had become inseparably linked in the mind of Gemma. She firmly believed that she would be a nun, if the new convent were founded within a given period of lime, beyond which her vocation could not be realized as the span of her life was short.

Such conditional dispositions of Divine Providence abound both in Scripture and in the lives of the saints. The prophet Jonas had announced the destruction of Ninive within forty days. Its citizens however hearkened to his words, fasted and covered their heads with ashes, thus averting the punishment with which their town had been threatened.[74] In a sermon preached at Salamanca, St. Vincent Ferrer foretold with the greatest assurance the imminent end of the world. As a proof of his prophetic veracity he there and then raised to life a woman dead for two days. His words created a stir and aroused the religious feeling throughout Europe. The end of the world did not come, but one wonders what its fate would have been had the warning of St. Vincent been allowed to pass unheeded.

Nearly all biographers of Gemma explain her persistent belief in a divine call to the religious life by adopting the theory of a supposed conditional vocation. Summing up all he had said on this point Father Germano remarks that: "(1) The desire of this holy maid to become a Passionist nun was for some years a sincere aspiration of her heart: (2) for a time, at least, she believed God wanted her to embrace that vocation; (3) this divine will, if it ever existed, was conditional depending, that is, upon events left to the free action of men; (4) toward the end of her life Gemma understood quite clearly in several revelations that she was to be a Passionist in spirit though a real nun of a better convent."

In reality, although Gemma felt and believed her vocation to be willed by God, yet the divine will is nowhere made the object of a clear revelation. Her correspondence on this subject is a little confusing. Consciously, or unconsciously, she uses different language when speaking of her personal feelings and when stating what she had heard in supernatural ecstasies. In the visions and apparitions of our Lord or St. Gabriel, various details of the new foundation are revealed to her, but she never speaks of any promise as to her becoming a Passionist. She says, quite candidly, that on being asked our Lord "smiled," and St. Gabriel called her "sister." There is a remarkable difference in the Letters and Ecstasies between the two series of revelations. Those concerning the convent are precise and definite in regard to time, persons, and similar details of the foundation. The others are vague, and make it by no means clear that her vocation to be a nun depended on the timely execution of God's design relating to the establishment of the new convent.

"It does not seem to me," says Gemma in a postscript to one of her letters, "that in speaking of the new convent Jesus tells me that I will be one of the nuns. I believe not. When I ask Him, He does not answer: He smiles."

She had at this time an apparition of our Blessed Lady, who sweetly embraced her and said among other consoling words: "Tell your Father that if he does not think of doing something for you, I will take you away to heaven." "I will ask Jesus to speak to you, Father," she says in reply to a letter from Father Germano, "you will understand what He tells you. To me He has never revealed the place where I must be."

There seems to be no necessity for postulating a special interference of God in Gemma's vocation to the religious life. It was, in the writer's opinion, a keen subjective desire which failed to become a reality because external circumstances stood in its way. Gemma was poor, enjoyed but indifferent health, and, strange as it may seem, was too highly favored by heaven to be a nun. She, moreover, had had enemies who at an earlier period of her life had prejudiced the nuns, those at least of Corneto, against her admission into their convent. However that may be, God, it seems, wanted her desire, not the deed. It is true that for a long time she firmly believed that Jesus wished her to enter the convent. How frequent and how persistent are her references to this subject. Had not Jesus repeatedly asked her to become a victim for the sins of mankind? But how could that be; how could she offer herself to divine immolation hindered by the restrictions of a dependent life? Both Monsignor Volpi and Father Germano were anxious that her extraordinary favors should be withdrawn from the public eye and the conversation of idlers. It were so easy to do so within the walls of a convent. One day our Lord asked her: "When shall I increase your sufferings?" She had no courage to answer. "If I had been a nun," she wrote, "I would promptly have said: 'Yes. Lord, double my pains and my sorrows' ... but in my circumstances what could I answer ... Oh, if I could but be alone to suffer ... there are other people to consider, how can I give them so much trouble?"

"Please, Father," she wrote, at about this time, to Father Germano, "make arrangements that I may make a retreat at Corneto in company with 'mamma' (Signora Cecilia). There I will pray Jesus to make them keep me." In fact Signora Cecilia herself wrote at once to the superioress: "Annetta, Euphemia (the two eldest Giannini girls) and myself, would like to come and make a retreat; there is also a young girl, an orphan, who stays with us, Gemma Galgani."

"But would you believe it," wrote Signora Cecilia to Father Germano, "the superioress replied that she could not allow her (Gemma) to come on account of the opposition of the nuns, who had heard a great deal of talk about her from different people. Just think of this poor girl who would have been so happy to go."

What the superioress had actually written was: "We will not have the convent contaminated by her," an expression which is surely as harsh as it was contemptuous. Gemma's humility, charity, and abandon under this hard blow were heroic. She had looked forward to making this retreat, and to see herself thus heartlessly rejected was a grief indeed. She could not restrain her tears, but there was not a shadow of resentment. "It is all the same, I shall make the retreat by myself," Gemma said, and spoke of it no more.

Finally, it was shown clearly to her in one of the last revelations that she had to renounce the hope of ever becoming a nun. She thus wrote to Father Germano about it:

"All is over. Last night at the midnight Mass, when the priest had reached the Offertory, I saw Jesus offer me as a victim to the Eternal Father, I was so happy, so contented, and then Jesus took me to our Mamma, and presented me to her, saying: 'This, My beloved daughter, must be regarded as the fruit of My Passion.' A little afterwards I went to receive Holy Communion. This morning I renewed my vows to Jesus. I besought Him to accept the renunciation of my desire, and to unite me to His Holy Passion."

Her self-denial was now complete and irrevocable. She never again speaks of her longing to be a nun, but waits for the fulfillment of the Savior's words that much suffering was in store for her and that He would soon take her to heaven. In a letter on this subject, we find a last allusion to the affair of the Passionists: "If they will not have me in life," she remarks, "they will have me in death" — a prophecy which came true to the letter, for after death Gemma was clothed in the dress of the Passionist nuns. Her body now rests and is venerated in the chapel of their convent outside the walls of Lucca.

The series of revelations relating to the foundation of a convent of Passionist nuns in Lucca, though inseparably joined in all Gemma's correspondence to the fact of her vocation, presents a much clearer evidence of divine intervention. Truly the nuns, who are now doing so much good, can claim to have been founded by the will and express command of heaven. The revelations that have reference to their institution are many. Nevertheless there is enough evidence for assigning the events we shall presently narrate to the last two years of the life of Gemma, that is, from the beginning of 1901 to the first months of 1903.

We shall begin with a revelation, which is clearly not the first chronologically, though it deserves the first place because of its importance and solemnity. Gemma herself declares she feels a repugnance in writing about it. In spite of an express command from our Lord she waits for more than ten days and adds with humility: "Even to Jesus I am disobedient." She had asked for prayers first to obtain the needed courage to write, and also that her director might receive light and grace to understand the words of the apparition.

"Since several days I feel so strongly the presence of Jesus after Holy Communion that it almost seems impossible to be able to stand it without dying. He also speaks to me of certain things which He alone can make me understand. Ten days ago, soon after Holy Communion, He said: 'Tell Me, daughter, do you love Me very much?' O, father, the quick movement of my heart gave answer. 'And if you love Me,' He commanded, 'you will do what I desire.' My heart answered for me, and Jesus said: 'It is an important matter, My daughter. You will have great things to tell your director. What ingratitude and wickedness there is in the world; sinners continue to live obstinately in their sins. The good people fall into confusion and despair. The fervent become tepid. The ministers of My sanctuary — (here Jesus was silent, and after some minutes continued). I have entrusted to them the great task of continuing My Redemption. ...' He was silent again. 'My Father can tolerate them no longer. He has continually given them light and strength, and they instead . . . these whom I have always held in predilection, whom I have always regarded as the apple of My eye ... (Jesus was silent and, as if it were, sighing). I receive nothing from creatures but ingratitude, and every day their indifference increases ...' Here Jesus continues to speak of the ever-growing evil in the world. 'I have need of souls who will give Me consolation. I have need of victims, strong victims in order to appease the just wrath of My Father ... My daughter, write at once to your father to speak of My desire to the Pope, tell him a great chastisement is threatening, and that I have need of victims. That My heavenly Father is exceedingly wroth. I assure you it will give great satisfaction to Me to have a new foundation of Passionist nuns in Lucca, thus increasing the number of souls that I can present to My Father to appease His indignation. Say also that these are My words and the last warning that I shall give.' "/5

Time passed rapidly by and nothing was being done to carry out the express command of our Lord. Gemma spoke to many persons, wrote letters, and to the best of her abilities collected funds for the new foundation. She had been saying three Hail Marys every day, for a Passionist Father who had asked of her this favor. One day Jesus said:

"Gemma, for whom did you pray?"

"For Father Francis."

"Did you speak to him of the new foundation?" "No, for in speaking of it he himself remarked that this was not a favorable time."

Then Jesus said smiling: "Tell Father Francis that heaven and earth shall pass; but My words shall not pass."

As might be expected it was St. Gabriel who in a special manner was interested in the work of the foundation. He appeared to her on several occasions. Once in a vision he asked:

"Gemma, have you nothing to tell me?"

"Oh, yes, much, also from the confessor. He wants to know about this convent which is to be, and who will begin the work; when it must be finished, and what time yet remains."

Here Gemma explains: "When I said this, I saw seven girls before me, and St. Gabriel made me look at each one. There were seven and I knew three of them."

"Who are these?" she asked.

"They will be Passionists," he said, and added: "Tell your confessor it is he who ought to begin this great work. Tell him to take courage. The devil will make a strong resistance, but what does it matter? Forward!"

"He was silent," Gemma continues her relation of this vision, "and then showed me a young girl and said: 'Look, this is she who will give the finishing stroke to the work. Do you know her?' 'No,' I replied. He told me her name and surname, and the city in which she was born and brought up; then all disappeared. I was rather in doubt about it all, but the vision was repeated three times and the third time St. Gabriel said: 'After two years have passed, on a Friday, the work will be begun.' "[76]

Sometime later, as it would seem, she writes: "After over three months, last evening, with the confessor's permission, I saw St. Gabriel, and with what power he spoke! His eyes flamed with fire, they seemed two burning lamps. He spoke at length about the new convent. How he laments that no one thinks about it, and yet soon, yes, within a year the work must be begun! You may do what you will but Jesus is thinking of it continually."[77]

In all these apparitions several persons were indicated who had to take part in the new foundation which the Holy Father himself was to approve and bless. Prominent among them stood Monsignor Volpi, as the principal mover in Lucca, while several Passionist Fathers were to give him help and assistance from Rome. But so far nobody had moved. Gemma's prayers, her industry in collecting funds, her numerous letters seemed for the time being utterly unsuccessful. Nobody minded her. Monsignor Volpi could do but little without the approval of the Archbishop, Monsignor Ghilardi, a man of great prudence who, being determined to take no risk, demanded a full dowry for every Sister of the new institution. In Rome nothing was being done, and the nuns of Corneto showed no interest in the matter. No one gave signs of that true and sincere confidence in God which impels the saints to start works of zeal in spite of adverse circumstances and human opposition.

"Father, you have understood?" writes Gemma in a letter where she describes an apparition of our Blessed Lady. "I live in much suffering, but in peace and quiet. I no longer ask to be received into the convent, as a better convent awaits me. I asked a sign of my dear Mamma that might assure me she was the Mother of God, and she said: 'I will restore you to health, that will make you sure.'" And in fact just after this Gemma recovered from a sickness from which she was suffering. But our Lady had put a condition to the cure: "Tell your Father I will give you health, but if he does not think of you, I shall take back my promise, and carry you off with me." The condition, it would seem, was not fulfilled and Gemma fell ill again. It was her last sickness, and of this she was to die, as we shall presently see. But we are anticipating events.

The death of the saints is usually accompanied by signs and prodigies. One by one the prophecies of Gemma began to come true with that inevitableness characteristic of the Divine Will. Father Germano was the first to feel inwardly moved to act. So far had he not resisted the express command of our Lord? Those words of Gemma, "Go to the Holy Father and tell him Jesus wishes this foundation," came back to his mind after Gemma's death with a new meaning and force. He went and opened his heart to Pope Pius X from whom he received the following letter:

With paternal love and affection we bless the new Convent of Passionist nuns in the city of Lucca; we bless our Venerable brother, the Archbishop Nicholas Ghilardi; the Reverend M. Maria Giuseppa of the Sacred Heart of Jesus, who will be first superior; the benefactors who have contributed and will contribute to its foundations and the Reverend Sisters of the Institution.

We wish that, in their prayers, penances and other spiritual practices prescribed by the rules, it be the object of the above mentioned Sisters to offer themselves victims to our Lord for the spiritual and temporal needs of the Church, and of the Holy Father.

Given at the Vatican,
October 2, 1903,
PIO PP. X.

Now that the Supreme Pontiff had in so many terms declared his will, things began to run more smoothly. Father Germano went to Lucca to take preliminary steps with the Archbishop and with the nuns of Corneto. Difficulties were bound to arise but they did not now appear insurmountable. On the death of Archbishop Ghilardi, Monsignor Volpi became Vicar-Capitular and Administrator of the Diocese. He immediately put his hands to the work God had assigned him. Things were shaping exactly in the way Gemma had foretold.

St. Gabriel had said that within a year the work would be begun, and in fact from the time of the vision to October 2, 1903, date of the Pontifical Decree, just one year had elapsed. On the other hand, in a previous apparition, he had told Gemma that the new Convent would be started two years after her death, on a Friday. The Sisters, who came to Lucca from Corneto to begin this foundation, left their convent on March 16, 1905, two years after Gemma's death, and entered Lucca on the following day, which was a Friday. Seven young girls were admitted as first novices; they were those seen and mentioned by Gemma. Of these, three only were known to her. She had also said that, although the new convent would begin two years after her death, it would be completed only a short time after the Beatification of Venerable Gabriel. This took place on May 31, 1908, and on July 31, of the same year, the Franciscan Fathers handed over the keys of their monastery to the Passionist nuns, to whom they had sold it sometime previously.

Thus God's will was being fulfilled in all the details as He had revealed it to His faithful servant, the angelic maid of Lucca.

Chapter XIX

THE BRIDE OF JESUS CRUCIFIED

Contemplation is the characteristic of mystical life, be it the gift of privileged souls or the legitimate aspiration and goal of all those who tend to perfection. In the ordinary or more common form of prayer, called meditation, the soul is usually active making full use of the powers of memory, intellect, and will. Often the meditation process implies arduous, uphill work, steady perseverance, as the consolations of prayer are tardy to come. Only by dint of faithful correspondence to grace through long years of personal endeavors does the spirit in meditation arrive to the fruition of peace and joy in the Lord.

In contemplation, on the other hand, the soul, though not necessarily raised from the first to an entirely passive state, yet finds itself more at rest even from the initial stages of its spiritual career. The Holy Ghost gives to it in greater abundance the gifts of wisdom and intellect. Thus enlightened from on high, the soul needs no reasonings of its own, no elaborate illustrations and reflections of the mind, but plunges at once into the sacred truths of heavenly things seeing and enjoying them, as it were, by intuition. In other words the contemplative is lifted by grace into the sight and fruition of God in a manner analogous to that which the Blessed possess in heaven by the light of glory.

Gemma's method of prayer has been recorded for us by Father Germano. She described it to him in her letters.

"I experience no difficulty or fatigue in my meditations," she says. "As I kneel before God to pray, my soul merges at once into the depths of divine mysteries and wanders in this paradise of incomprehensible beauty and ineffable truths. It flies into the bosom of the Godhead, leaving the material body here on earth. I find myself suddenly in the presence of Jesus and am lost in Him. An ardent love for the divine Lover seems to seize me, and the more I gaze on Him, the sweeter I find Him and the more lovable. At times Jesus appears as if radiant with the light of an eternal, uncreated Sun. It is the splendor of God Almighty to whom every created thing is subject, whose will is power and whose power is will."

On being asked by the director whether she saw Jesus with bodily eyes, she replied:

"When I begin to pray I do not see Jesus with the eyes of the body, but I know He is there before me, and my soul finds rest in His presence. I hear His voice which at times is as piercing as a sword, and penetrates into the inner senses of my spirit. His words are words of life. When I see Him in this manner and hear His voice, it is not a beautiful corporeal form that I see, nor do I hear the sound of a human voice, but I see a light great, infinite, and hear a voice inarticulate yet strong, which to the soul is more powerful than the loudest sound of storm or wind."

And again she writes: "Father, try to think of a light that fills the whole universe, that penetrates and kindles it and, at the same time, gives life and animation to all things so that all things which exist are imbued with, or encircled in this light, and in it and through it have life. Thus I see God and in Him all creatures. He is a burning fire. It burns but does not consume, on the contrary, it gives light and warmth and joy, and the more it burns, the more happy and perfect it makes those encircled by its rays, and the more anxious do they become to be burning in His fire. Thus do I see the souls in God."

In the same mystical strain she spoke of the mystery of the Blessed Trinity, and plunged into the ocean of mystical theology with such clearness of thought as to draw the admiration of those around her. Monsignor Volpi himself gave evidence of the deep impression these revelations of Gemma made upon him. Once the Reverend J. Ghilardi, then her parish priest, was present at an ecstasy of Gemma. He testified that she so profoundly discussed the mystery of the Blessed Trinity that, turning to Signora Cecilia, he said: "Has this girl made any special study of theological subjects, or is she in the habit of reading books on mysticism?"

The events we are now going to narrate occurred sometime during the year 1902. Once while she was rapt in ecstasy, Jesus appeared to Gemma in the form of a lovely child in its mother's arms. The Blessed Mother took a ring from His finger and placed it on that of Gemma, who, wholly rapt out of her senses, gave way to a most seraphic outburst of love. We shall give the speech in full. It has been called inspired by some writers and, in the original text, has found a place in anthologies among the classical passages of Italian literature.

"But what is this I feel? I cannot, O my true God, yield myself up to this sweetness, this happiness ... What is this, I feel, my God! Thine are the saints and humble of heart; not I, O Lord. Thine the souls of all the just, not I, Lord. All the inhabitants of heaven are Thine, not I. May they all render Thee infinite praise and thanksgiving. But I, O Jesus, yes, even I — wretched unworthy sinner — want to love Thee, and with a unique love. Help me, my Strength. Fire! there is fire in my heart! It is aflame this morning. Give me words that I may, day and night, speak only of Thy glory, and love Thee forever and ever. Unclean are my lips and my whole body is unclean. I need Thee, I want Thee to cleanse me from every stain. Sanctify me, Jesus. In Thy mind, in Thy sweetness let my soul dwell forever. Lift me from visible things up to the invisible, from earthly things up to the heavenly.

"O, my God, my Jesus! ... Jesus, what sayest Thou? O, true Love, Thou art my God; toward Thee I feel forever moved, forever drawn, and wish to be united to Thee! When I am near Thee, I live; away from Thee I languish and perish. It is the Faith that so teaches me, the Faith Thou hast put into my heart to enlighten my path. May we all know Thee, my God, and knowing Thee know the Truth and Eternity ... Who is like unto Thee, O God: who is like unto Thee? Thou art the omnipotent God. My Jesus, true Love, Thou art my God!

"Jesus, my Redeemer, I bless and praise Thee, my soul gives Thee infinite thanks, yet surely Jesus, far below all Thy goodness to me ... It gives Thee thanks, not as it ought, but as it can in its wretchedness and poverty ... Take me, Jesus, into Thy infinite mercy ... I offer Thee praise and prayers: receive them that I may be less unworthy of the favor done to me this morning. Thy goodness has made me; Thy mercy has redeemed me, Thy infinite patience suffers me.

"Thou, O Jesus, art waiting for my repentance, and I long for Thy inspiration to begin a new life. My soul wants Thee, O Jesus ... it needs Thee ... To love Thee truly, I shall bear in mind Thy sufferings, Thy Sacred Wounds, Thy death and cross and resurrection ... but, above all, Thy ascension.

"Why was I not present on the day of Thy ascension? Why was I not there to see an offended God speak with sinners? ... And Thou didst go about, my sweet Consoler, blessing all that were with Thee; but I was not there ... Thy hands were raised in benediction, and a cloud brought Thee up into the sky. The Angels said Thou wouldst return; but I saw Thee no more. Yet Thou wilt return, for Thou art ... my life, my prop, my strength ... the strength of my arms. Come, Jesus, and be the king of my heart.

"What are, O Lord, all the consolations of the earth without Thee? Yes, Jesus, let me hear Thy voice, let me hear but one word as Thou didst speak in the days of trial. Mayest Thou be blessed, Jesus, for Thou hast taken all creatures from me that I may be closer to Thee. Ah! Thou art the consoler, Thou alone and none other. What does it matter if I have no consolations in this world? Thou art enough for me. What does it matter if all were to despise me? Thou remainest, who canst console me.

Oh, had I understood this earlier, and abandoned myself earlier into Thy arms. Yet, if Thou art so good to me, a sinner, what wilt Thou be to the pure of heart, to the saints?

"Jesus, let me come to Thee. I knew Thou wert my only Good, and yet ... I was drawn to unworthy creatures. What hope had I? Perhaps to find in them more riches and pleasures? Forgive my wretchedness and my sinfulness; may I never more feel tired of Thy love. May I never repay Thy love with my ingratitude. What were to me the petty consolations of this world, O Jesus, without Thy consolations?

"Thou alone, Jesus, canst still the tempest that now and then rises in my heart; Thou alone canst strengthen my soul; Thou alone. For though alone, Thou art omnipotent."[78]

Like all the revelations of the world's prophets and seers, these spiritual effusions of Gemma Galgani come to us with perfect accuracy of diction and ideas. They seem to challenge the most learned, the most rigorous criticism of mystical theology. This is a proof, if any be needed, of the veracity of her supernatural experiences as a whole. It may be difficult to draw a sharp dividing line between one phenomenon and another, and to assign to each, and part of each, its full share of natural or supernatural origin. It is but secondary matter about which any number of people may very reasonably debate and differ. What really matters, what the Church has implied by Gemma's glorification, what her life teaches, is that by these inner experiences, strange though many of them may seem, the maiden of Lucca takes her place side by side with the great mystics of the Church.

It was remarked that from the days of her espousals, Gemma seemed no longer a being of earth. That majesty of countenance which had always distinguished her, the splendor of the eyes, the sweet smile upon the lips, and all else that adorned her, were henceforth transfigured into something ethereal which exacted reverence from all around. Writing to Father Germano about this new state, she said:

"Jesus continues to be so loving with me, but not in the same way as of old when I was a child. He unites and gathers me to Himself in a new way."

Chapter XX

THE PASSING OF GEMMA

From the time of her miraculous cure, if we leave out of account some occasional indispositions of no serious consequence, Gemma continued, on the whole, to enjoy good health. This has been attested by Signora Cecilia who was much surprised at it, knowing full well the small amount of food Gemma was taking, her frequent loss of blood, her severe interior trials, the contradictions of misguided neighbors and the assaults of the evil spirit. There seemed in fact no reason to think that Gemma's days would soon draw to a close.

On the Feast of the Ascension, 1902, as we surmise, she received those extraordinary communications of which we spoke in the preceding chapter. Already for some time a sense of immolation in her spiritual outlook had produced a corresponding change in her external attitude to life. It could not escape the notice of those around her. In a letter to the spiritual director, Signora Cecilia remarks that Gemma's deep piety had blossomed, like a flower of grace in deeds and prayers, and adds:

"You cannot look her in the face, she seems a seraph; when you have gazed at her for a while, you are forced to lower your eyes through reverence. She prefers to be alone, is more silent, more serious than heretofore, and withal she takes part in her domestic work as of old. At prayer she appears to be always in ecstasy. If you saw her, you would be moved to tears. If only I could repeat the words of fire welling from the lips of our darling Gemma!"

It was during this latter period of her life that our Saint experienced in a spiritual manner the pains of scourging, the crowning with thorns and the three hours' agony of our Lord. The event is testified by reliable witnesses who saw her during an ecstasy, trembling in every limb, whilst blood flowed from her head. For three hours her countenance seemed that of one plunged in a veritable ocean of pain.

Finally, on the day of Pentecost, in one of her last recorded visions, our Lord appeared to claim the consummation of that sacrifice of herself which she had already offered Him for the conversion of sinners and in particular in atonement for the sins of many priests. He said: "I have need of a great expiation, especially for the sacrileges with which I am offended by the ministers of My sanctuary. Were it not for the angels who assist at my throne many of them would be stricken dead by the avenging justice of My Father." And when the heavenly Bridegroom, turning to Gemma, asked her if she would become a victim for these sins, she answered with the impetuous force of passionate love: "Yes, Jesus, Jesus, I embrace it! Yes. Jesus, at once sacrifice me, and be glorified in Your miserable creature."

The generous offering, which characterizes the mission of her life on earth and of her sanctity, even from the days when, as a little child, she longed to pay monthly her small contribution to the association of the Holy Infancy, was accepted, and Gemma fell grievously ill. Her stomach closed up. She could no longer take any food, or if she attempted to swallow any, it gave her no relief, but seemed to choke her until she rejected it again. For two months her entire nourishment consisted almost exclusively of a little wine. It was a wonder to many how she could at all live. No one was able to discover the nature of her illness or the cause of the strange phenomena which accompanied it. Father Germano, knowing her secret, and unwilling that she should put herself into the hands of the physicians, bade her to pray for recovery. Gemma, not without doing great violence to herself, obeyed and asked our Lord to give her the desired grace. In a week she was restored to health, but Jesus told her that the relief would not be of long duration. On September 9 she had a relapse, and on the twenty-first day of the same month she fell into a fever and threw up blood, which this time came from the lungs. To add to her affliction, God now seemed to leave her to herself, and seldom sent her those heavenly communications and miraculous favors which were precious as testifying to His presence and special care of her.

In October Father Germano was urgently called from Rome to the bedside of Gemma by a pressing letter from Signora Cecilia. We can easily imagine the joy and consolation which his visit brought to the long-suffering girl. The good Father on his part was grieved at the change he saw in her, and having given her his blessing he sat by the bedside.

"And now, Gemma," he asked her, "what is to be done?" "I am going to heaven, Father, to Jesus," she answered. "Indeed!" he rejoined.

"Yes, Father." And she continued, "This time Jesus has told me so, oh, how plainly!"

"But what of your sins, will they not be a hindrance?"

"Jesus has thought of that," she answered. "He will make me suffer so much during the little time I have still to live, and will so sanctify my poor sufferings with the merit of His Passion, that His Justice will be satisfied, and He will take me with Him to heaven."

"But I do not wish you to die now," objected the Father.

"But if Jesus does, what then?" she wistfully replied.

At Gemma's own request, he allowed her that evening to make once more her general confession. "It was for the last time," he writes, "and I could hardly restrain tears of consolation at the conviction of what I already knew, namely, that throughout her course of twenty-five years, she had never been guilty of even a single deliberate venial sin, and that she was carrying with her unstained the fair garment of baptismal innocence."

It was Father Germano's intention to remain for some time in Lucca, one reason being that he might be of consolation to his penitent in her last moments. But Providence had decreed otherwise. A few days after his arrival at Lucca he received an order from Rome, recalling him on some urgent business to the Eternal City. Before leaving he thought it well, in the interest of the health of the younger members of the family, that precautionary measures should be taken. The physicians were divided in opinion as to the nature of Gemma's malady. Some held that it was tubercular phthisis, others that it was a strange and mysterious disease, but all agreed that there was possibility of infection. Accordingly Father Germano recommended that she should be isolated, but so unwilling were the Gianninis to part with their beloved guest that three months were allowed to pass before the step was taken.

One day Monsignor Tei, who afterwards became Bishop of Pesaro, wishing perhaps to put to the test the virtue of this holy girl, said:

"Gemma, the doctors say you are consumptive and they are telling those of the house to send you away."

"My present sickness is not consumption," replied Gemma, "but they do well to remove me from the children."

"Where will you go?" asked the priest. "Without money nothing but the street remains to you."

"Oh, Father," replied Gemma, "is not God even in the streets?"

Meanwhile the girl's malady ran its natural course with those variations which, from day to day, gave rise alternately to hopes and fears. The doctors held further consultations as a result of which they insisted on the immediate removal of the patient from the contact of so many children. Gemma was calm and anxious to go away, but felt the separation from a family between whose inmates and herself there had sprung up the tenderest human affection. They, too, and especially Signora Cecilia could not brook the idea of leaving Gemma. "If she must die," they said, "we will take care of her till the last."

Finally one of Gemma's aunts hired apartments in a house close by, the windows of which commanded a view of the house she was leaving. So, then, on January 24, 1903, the patient was removed to the new quarters. She wept and could not help exclaiming: "This is the second time that I have lost my mother. May Jesus be praised; alone with Jesus only."

To add to her perfect immolation, it pleased God to withdraw all extraordinary gifts — the stigmata and ecstasies, the visions and spiritual consolations. Like a true soldier of Christ she was to fight the final battle all alone.

"Even the memory of past favors," she wrote to Father Germano, "has disappeared and I no longer feel that sweet presence of Jesus which has been from my very childhood the strength and main support of my life."

Despite the fever Gemma managed to rise every morning and drag herself to the neighboring church. Even in her circumstances it was easy to pray there; to sink into the depths of mystical contemplation when, as happens between human lovers, there is no more need of words, and thought itself merges into union of the soul with God.

On the other hand, the devil redoubled his attacks. He set before her, under its most depressing aspects, the picture of her sorrowful life: the death of father and mother, the misfortunes of her family and her own incessant sufferings; he suggested that she was entirely forsaken by God and on the brink of everlasting perdition. "See," he would whisper, "see the fruit of your many prayers, Masses, and Communions." Often he appeared in most hideous forms. Sometimes in the likeness of a snake he would coil around her body; at others, he would assume the shape of a mad dog or other animal, filling the room with sounds and strange unearthly noises.

"I came away from our Gemma in tears," wrote one of the Giannini girls who was helping to nurse the dying child, "because the devil is wearing her out, and the wretch will surely cause her death. We all joined in sprinkling holy water in the room; then for a moment the disturbances ceased, but only to begin again a little later even worse than before."

"Poor martyr," said Signora Cecilia, speaking of these last days of Gemma, "poor victim of Jesus. She suffers without the least respite, and feels her very bones being disjointed. She is tortured in each and every part of the body and is gradually being dissolved in terrible agony."

Many never know what it means to come in contact with the hard reality of death until they reach maturity. Not so with our Saint. By the loss of father and mother she had found herself face to face with the mystery of death almost before she had known the joy of life. She was quite prepared for it and, in spite of pain and suffering, endeavored to express her gratitude for any small service with that charming smile that never left her. She never complained, nor asked for relief, never gave a sign of feeling wearied or depressed. Euphemia Giannini, her bosom friend and sharer of her intimate secrets, testified that "never throughout her illness did she ask us even for a drop of water."

Her only occupation, during the two months that still remained, was to pray. And from prayer she ever came consoled, as one who has looked upon the face of God and has therein found peace and consolation. Hence it was that in spite of temporary darkness in the soul and desolation of the spirit, she still turned to our Lord as in the days of joy, asking Him: "Where are You, my Jesus, where are You?"

To one of the nuns of St. Camillo de Lellis, who had been invited to nurse her, she said, "Let us pray, Sister, let us pray always. We must not think of anything but Jesus." Those that watched by her bedside are unanimous in saying that her only consolation during the long, sleepless nights, was to place herself, in thought and love, on Calvary. She whispered the name of Jesus Crucified as long as her lips had strength to move, and turned to Him in thought when the voice completely failed her. Once only she said: "Jesus, I can bear no more," but because the Sister reminded her that with God's grace we can do all things, she resolved never to use that exclamation again. When, on one occasion, somebody touched with pity remarked thereafter: "Poor thing: she can bear no more," Gemma instantly replied: "Yes, I can still bear a little more for the love of God."

At another time a Sister said: "Gemma, if the choice were left to you, to go at once to heaven and have done with so much suffering, or to remain here and continue to suffer if this contributes to the glory of God, which would you choose?" Gemma immediately answered: "Far better to remain here and suffer for Jesus, if it gives Him glory."

On Wednesday in Holy Week, Gemma was in her last agony. Outside, the sky was glorious. The early clouds of the morning had melted away in the warm rays of the Italian sun which filled the town with light and life. But in one little room, high in a garret, Gemma lay in her bed of sickness; the pallor of death had already overspread her countenance and she remained motionless as one who awaits the signal to depart. Suddenly, once more, she fell into ecstasy and exclaimed: "Jesus, Jesus!" but soon returning to herself she said to the Sister: "Oh, Sister, if only you could see the smallest particle of that which Jesus has shown me, how you would rejoice."

Later, during the same day, she was administered Holy Viaticum and, on the morrow, Maundy Thursday, she desired once more to receive Communion. To be more easily allowed to do so, she willingly kept the fast notwithstanding the burning fever which consumed her. The rest of the time was spent wholly in the contemplation of the Saving Death of Christ and in preparation for the following Good Friday.

At ten o'clock of that hallowed day, Signora Cecilia, feeling exhausted with fatigue and lack of sleep, wanted to go home to take a little rest. The dying girl said to her:

"Do not leave me until I am nailed to the Cross. I must be crucified with Jesus, is it not Friday? Jesus has told me that His children must be crucified."

Soon afterwards, the Saint entered into ecstasy. She gradually extended her arms, and remained in this posture until half past one. Her pale countenance showed sorrow and love, calmness and desolation, all blended in one.

Toward eight o'clock on Holy Saturday morning, the priest came to administer the Sacrament of Extreme Unction, which Gemma received with fervent devotion, endeavoring to answer the prayers as far as her feeble voice permitted it. She was still suffering much in body and in soul, and expressed a desire to speak to Monsignor Volpi, her ordinary confessor from early childhood. The Monsignor, who was busy with the long functions of those hallowed days, replied he had no time to see her. On receiving this answer Gemma smiled feebly; then raising her eyes to a picture of the Madonna on the wall, said: "My Mamma, I commend my soul to you. Tell Jesus to be merciful unto me."

She lingered on for yet a little while. At about midday. Monsignor Volpi had just time to pay a hasty visit. He blessed her, but left almost immediately, promising to return toward evening. It proved too late. Speaking of it afterwards he said: "I found her in great suffering, physically as well as spiritually, but fully resigned. I gave her absolution and left her in a very bad state, but in perfect tranquility of spirit."

Shortly after the confessor's departure, Gemma was heard to say: "Jesus, I commend my soul to You, my Jesus!" They were the last words she uttered. For about half an hour she remained seated on her bed, her head resting on the shoulder of Signora Giustina. The other members of the Giannini family had been called in and remained around her, kneeling. All at once, a heavenly smile played about Gemma's lips, a ray of the sun illumined her face. Letting her head gently fall to one side, she quietly ceased to breathe, while the bells of the Cathedral were pealing forth the last joyous notes of the Resurrection.

It was about one o'clock of Holy Saturday, April 11, 1903.

"She looks like an angel." Such were the words of those who stood around Gemma in the hour of her death. The Sisters of St. Camillo de Lellis, knowing how she had longed to be a Passionist nun, clothed her in that habit, placing the rosary around her neck and the badge of the Passion on her breast.

As the rumor of Gemma's death spread through the city of Lucca, a large concourse of people kept streaming in, all day and all night, to pray by the side of her lifeless remains. Greater still was the concourse on Easter Sunday, when early in the morning the body of Gemma Galgani was carried in funeral procession to the grave. Over the tomb was put up a Latin inscription which says:

> Gemma Galgani of Lucca, a most innocent virgin, who, consumed rather by the fire of divine love than by disease, in the twenty-fifth year of her age, went forth to her heavenly espousals on the eleventh of April, 1903, this being the vigil of our Lord's Resurrection. Peace be to thee, sweet soul, in the company of Angels.

Appendix

The fame of Gemma's sanctity spread almost miraculously not only throughout Italy but over all the Catholic world. Her precious remains were first consigned to the earth in the civic cemetery, then transferred to the Church of the Passionists outside Porta Elisa, in Lucca. Both these places soon became centers of pilgrimage. Many graces were obtained and many miracles wrought through her intercession.

Between the years 1907 and 1910, the preliminary diocesan inquiries (*Processi informativi*) into her virtues were held at Lucca. In 1922 the canonical process began, which lasted long and entered into the minutest details of Gemma's life. November 29, 1931, witnessed, in the presence of the Holy Father, the reading of the decree declaring her virtues heroic. It became permissible from that day to call her "Venerable Gemma Galgani." On January 5, 1933, Pope Pius XI approved the two miracles proposed for the Beatification, and finally, on Sunday, May 14, of the same year, she was raised to the honors of the Altar. Her canonization has been scheduled for May, 1940.

Soon after the solemnities of the Beatification the fame of new miracles, attributed to the intercession of Blessed Gemma Galgani, spread all over Italy. People were thus reminded of the words of our Lord to our Saint: "Within a few years, by My special grace, you will be a saint, you will work miracles and will be raised to the honors of the altar" (*Posit, super scriptis,* p. 23). From various parts of the world prayers and requests were addressed to the Holy See asking for the canonization of the new Blessed.

Out of a large number of miracles two were selected to be submitted for examination to the Sacred Congregation of Rites presided over by His Eminence Cardinal Januario Granito Pignatelli di Belmonte, Promoter of the Cause.

The investigation of these two miracles fills three folio volumes. It were out of place to give here the details of the examination, which furnishes an eloquent proof, if any be needed, of the care and diligence habitual to the Church before accepting miracles proposed to her for approval.

I Miracle. Elisa Scarpelli of Lappano, in South Italy, was a young girl who had always enjoyed good health. At the beginning of September, 1932, when she was but ten years old, she developed a tubercle on the left jaw. After a few days there appeared on the same jaw a cluster of swollen glands. For two months the people at home made light of the matter. Considering it an ordinary swelling, they punctured it with a needle. This made the tubercle turn into a festering ulcer. The girl was taken to Dr. Augustine Intrieri who first applied a linseed poultice; he then resorted to a surgical operation in which accidentally he touched the festering glands. These, as well as the adenoids, soon became running sores, and no means could be found to heal the ulcers which grew more malignant during the next five months. The girl was then taken to another doctor, Signor Francesco Guido, who applied better remedies but with no better results. The poor sufferer was also examined by still two more doctors who agreed in diagnosing the malady as a cutaneous tuberculosis with lesion of the facial gland which had developed into an abscess in the latero-cervical region of the left jaw. Their common opinion was that such a noxious abscess could not long remain without affecting the general health of the patient.

On the morning of Sunday, May 14, the day on which Gemma Galgani was beatified, Elisa Scarpelli, disregarding the warnings of her mother, went to church to hear Mass. On reaching home, having heard that perhaps at that very moment Gemma Galgani was glorified, she withdrew to her room. There she took a picture of the new Blessed and, in an impetus of hope and faith, removed the bandages, applying the picture to the ulcers, which were running matter as usual. "Gemma, look at me and have pity on my condition; cure me," she meanwhile prayed. After this prayer she looked with great expectations into the mirror and saw that the wounds had healed and the skin had regained its natural color, as in the other jaw. Immediately she called to her mother, who also witnessed the fact that the swelling of the glands had disappeared. The wounds had healed, and the color had become normal.

II Miracle. The facts which follow took place in the same village of Lappano. The person in question was a farmer who bore the surname of the recipient of the previous miracle. He was Noel Scarpelli, who with the labor of his hands had to provide for the maintenance of his little family, which consisted of his wife and a daughter.

In 1918, when thirty years old, Noel Scarpelli began to suffer from varicose veins. For ten long years he patiently bore his malady. At the end of this period he was forced to undergo an operation. This was so far successful as to enable him to attend to his farming in the vast fields of the Sila region (Southern Italy). Unfortunately, on April 3, 1935, he happened to knock his left leg severely against a large trunk. This caused a laceration of the skin, which, after being neglected for over a month, turned into an ulcer. Finally, on May 18, Noel Scarpelli was obliged to betake himself to Cosenza to consult Dr. Valentini, in whom he greatly confided. The doctor said nothing to the patient, but understood it was a clear case of varicose ulcer and prescribed the first remedies, inclusive of absolute rest in bed.

But the patient could not afford to miss his daily work, on which alone depended the maintenance of his family. Moreover, as it appeared later, the prescriptions of Dr. Valentini were not the best. The wounds grew worse, and in the end the patient had to betake himself to his bed. His general physical condition grew worse every day. The wound began to run matter and to spread very fast. The gravity of the disease, at this point, is amply testified by the doctors appointed by the Sacred Congregation for the examination of the miracle. Poor Scarpelli was in fact suffering acute pains in the leg and began to fear he would never be able to work again in his fields. This was also the opinion of his fellow workers, who no longer expected to see him again in the vast farms of the Sila.

It was a terrible blow for the poor family that had subsisted only by the daily wages of the father. He himself was greatly downcast as he saw no prospect of a radical cure. One day his daughter, to console him a little, said: "Papa, let us invoke Blessed Gemma — she has recently worked a miracle for our neighbor Elisa; why should she not work one for us also?"

Both Scarpelli and his wife felt greatly encouraged at these words and promised to proclaim the miracle should it occur. The three together then fervently recited a prayer to Blessed Gemma imploring the desired grace. At the end of the prayer Noel's daughter took the relic of the Blessed and with it made a sign of the cross on the wound. Then instead of again bandaging the wound with plaster, she applied only a clean gauze asking in her heart that as a token of the cure wrought by the Blessed, the gauze should not stick to the wound. The bandaging over Noel Scarpelli, who had been seated on the bed during the prayer, lay down full length. A few minutes afterwards he felt unusually well and laughingly said to his daughter: "Why did you not think of placing the relic on the leg long before?" Having uttered these words he quietly and comfortably fell asleep, a thing he had not been able to do for several days. Meanwhile his daughter withdrew also to her room to sleep, and after a short prayer to Blessed Gemma, went to rest full of confidence. Praise be to God, though unnoticed by anyone, the miracle had taken place the very moment the relic had been applied.

In fact, the following morning, when the gauze was removed they saw the cloth as clean as when it had been applied, with no trace of pus. More marvelous still, the wound had completely healed, the cavity was filled and covered over with fresh skin up to the level of the surrounding tissues. Yet, strange to say, the varicose veins persisted, but with no pain in the leg so that the farmer was able to attend to his hard work without the use of any bandage or elastic sock and with perfect freedom of movement.

To realize the greatness of the miracle performed by Blessed Gemma we might conclude with the words of an expert who had to examine the case: "This healing is not only incomprehensible but upsets all the physi-opathological laws, even the most fundamental, of the medical field, and contrasts with the usual working of the natural laws. For let us remember that between a varicose ulcer and an ordinary wound there exists a veritable abyss of difference" (Dr. Jacobelli).

After a most elaborate and minute examination, these two miracles were submitted for the final approval to the Holy Father, on December 8, 1938. *"Tuum namque est,"* says the Cardinal Promoter to the Holy Father, *"inerrabili oraculo de veritate prodigiorum, deque illustri B. Gemmae sanctitate decernere."*

Endnotes

[1] *"Itlud perstat cunctis spectabile vitae exemplum, quo humilis haec puella dilabenti in vanitatem mundo Jesum praedicaverit et hunc Crucifixum"*

[2] St. Gemma Galgani is one of the Patrons of the Catholic Pharmaceutical Guild in England.

[3] The following are the names of the children born to the Galganis: Guido born May 30, 1871, died June 19, 1922; Ettore, born March 21, 1873, died in 1927; Gino, born June 5, 1876, died September, 1894; Gemma Maria, born March 12, 1878, died April 11, 1903; Antonio, born March 14, 1880, died October 21, 1902; Angela, born September, 1881; Giulia, born October 30, 1883, died August 19, 1902.

[4] One of the glories of Lucca, and not the least, is its connection with St. Francis of Assisi. According to a document discovered by Bishop Spader in the eighteenth century, the family of St. Francis, the Bernardoni, had migrated to Assisi from Lucca. Cf. *Life of St. Francis of Assisi*, Cuthbert, p. 15.

[5] "Episiola estis Christi" (2 Cor. 3:3).

[6] *Autobiography*, p. 12.

[7] Ps. 41:2.

[8] *La Beata Gemma Galgani*, by Sister Gesualda of the Holy Ghost, p. 23, note.

[9] *Autobiography*, p. 14.

[10] *Letter LXIV*. Gemma often passes in her letters from one form of speech to another: from the narrative to the direct discourse, following the promptings of her heart, quite unmindful of the rules of grammar and style. The letters were surely not meant for publication.

[11] P. Germano of St. Stanislaus, *Biography of the Venerable Gemma Galgani*, p. 35.

[12] *La Beata Gemma Galgani*, by Rev. Fr. Amedeo, C.P., p. 22.

[13] Luke 1:66.

[14] Process for the Beatification. Deposition by Guido Galgani.

[15] Joergensen, *Life of St. Catherine of Siena*.

[16] *Autobiography*, pp. 35, 36.

[17] *Autobiography*, pp. 38, 39.

[18] At this time St. Gabriel had not yet been canonized. The canonization took place in 1920.

[19] *Life of St. Francis*, by Cuthbert, O.S.F.C., Bk. IV, Ch. 3.

[20] *Autobiography*, p. 49.

[21] *Ibid.*, p. 50 seq.

[22] Strange enough, this idea of sinfulness recurs over and over again in her correspondence with Father Germano. It is, in fact, a prominent feature of the letters.

[23] Reverend Father Germano of St. Stanislaus, C.P., of whom more will be said hereafter, was Gemma's spiritual director during the last three years of her life. The letters alluded to were published by him in the volume entitled: *Lettere ed Estasi*. The edition used by the writer is that of 1924.

[24] *Letter XLVI.*

[25] Matthew Arnold somewhere in one of his books, calls this line one of the most sublime in the world's literature.

[26] *Autobiography*, pp. 73, 74.

[27] *Ibid.*, p. 83.

[28] St. Bonaventure, *Leg. Maj.* xiii, 3. *"Quodam mane circa festum Exaltationis sanctae crucis."*

[29] From the *Life of St. Francis of Assisi*, by Father Cuthbert, O.S.F.O., Book iv, Chaps. 1 and 2.

[30] Letter of Brother Elias to Gregory of Naples to announce the death of St. Francis. Father Cuthbert, Introduction to the *Life of St. Francis of Assisi*.

[31] *Catholic Encyclopedia*. See article "Stigmata."

[32] Gal. 6:14.

[33] *Autobiography*, pp. 56-60.

[34] *Ibid.*, pp. 76-78.

[35] *Gemma of Lucca*, by Father Williamson, p. 59.

[36] "Le Camus in his *Life of Christ* says that there were two ways of crucifying the condemned. They were attached to the cross sometimes by ropes, sometimes by nails. Both the one and the other way were used in Jesus' time. We know from the Gospel (John 20:25) that our Lord was nailed to the cross. It is perhaps simply for the sake of contrast that artists sometimes represent the thieves as bound to their crosses. Similarly they represent the crosses of the thieves as lower than that of Christ, although probably all three were alike. St. Helena, in fact, did not recognize the Cross of Christ from the crosses of the thieves. It is not known whether our Lord's feet were fastened by a single nail or two. A writer on Christian iconography says that previous to the 13th century painters represented Christ on the Cross sometimes with three nails, sometimes with four, but that since that date only three nails have generally been admitted. One of the nails, said to have been found by St. Helena, is venerated in Rome." (From *Examiner*, March 17, 1934.)

[37] *Summ. Proc. super virtutibus*, p. 55

[38] *Biography of the Venerable Gemma Galgani*, by Father Germano, p. 361.

[39] See Father Williamson's *Gemma of Lucca*, p. 77. Sister Gesualda gives a different account. She says that the manuscript, in answer to the prayer of Gemma, was not submitted to the specialist and cites the authority of Father Germano. *La Beata Gemma Galgani*, p. 199.

[40] *Autobiography*, pp. 91, 92; *Life* by Father Germano, p. 124.

[41] This letter is not to be found in the volume *Lettere ed Estasi.* What Father Williamson calls "second letter" is in reality the first in the volume. The first one must have been lost or awaits a more complete edition of the *Lettere ed Estasi.* Even incomplete as it is the volume of the letters is called by the Civiltá Catholica a treasure of heavenly wisdom. (Civiltá Catholica, 1909, Vol. II, p. 727.)

[42] Gen. 32:26.

[43] The remaining portion of this chapter is taken almost entirely from Father Williamson's *Gemma of Lucca* (p. 90). The facts are originally narrated by Father Germano.

[44] *Gemma Galgani*, by Philip Coghlan, C.P., pp. 32, 33.

[45] Phil. 11:8.

[46] *Gemma Galgani*, by Philip Coghlan. C.P., p. 42.

[47] *La Beata Gemma Galgani*, by Sister Gesualda of the Holy Ghost, p. 47.

[48] From various Letters especially from *Letter XXV.*

[49] *Catholic Encyclopedia*, "Ecstasy."

[50] Jeanne Danemarie, *The Mystery of Stigmata.*

[51] *Gemma Galgani*, by Philip Coghlan, C.P., p. 57 seq.

[52] *Lettere ed Estasi della Serva di Dio Gemma Galgani*, Roma, 1924.

[53] *Summ. Proc. super virtutibus*, pp. 771, 772.

[54] From *Lettere ed Estasi.*

[55] Matt. 18:10.

[56] Heb. 1:14.

[57] Ps. 90:11.

[58] *The Holy Angels*, by R. O'Kennedy, p. 100.

[59] Newman, *Apologia*.

[60] St. Thomas, Quaest. 12, *De Veritate*, art. 8.

[61] 1 Pet. 5:8.

[62] John 8:44.

[63] Luke 11:10.

[64] Eph. 6:12.

[65] Milton, *Paradise Lost*, Bk. 2.

[66] Tob. 12:13.

[67] *Letter XXVII.* Unfortunately like all other letters it is undated.

[68] *Letter XXVIII.*

[69] B. Williamson, *Gemma of Lucca*, pp. 158, 159.

[70] *La Beata Gemma Galgani*, by Father Amedeo, C.P., p. 240.

[71] *Letter XXXVIII.*

[72] Job 1:6.

[73] Corneto was the only place in Italy where there was a convent of Passionist nuns.

[74] John 3:4.

[75] This revelation we reprint, with few verbal changes, from Father Williamson's *Life of Gemma*. The full text, of which this is an abridgment, is published in *Letter LII* of the *Letters and Ecstasies*.

[76] Letter *LIII*.

[77] *Letter LV*. We shall presently see how all these prophecies came true to the letter even to the apparent difference about the time.

[78] *Lettere ed Estasi*, Roma, 1924. "Estasi XXXIII." It seems clear from the context, that this ecstasy either occurred on Ascension Day, or was prompted by a meditation on that mystery. It bears all the marks, and contains all the parts of a model meditation.

Made in the USA
Las Vegas, NV
03 January 2023

64729169R00118